MAS

QB20

The Undiscovered Country

The reason we climb

'Wherever nature has raised a bump above the plain it has meant something. Wherever migrating peoples have crossed high passes they have left signs there, flags streaming in the wind.'
The summit of the Langma La, Tibet, with the north side of Makalu and Chomolonzo in the background.
(Photo: Stephen Venables, 1988.)

THE UNDISCOVERED COUNTRY

The reason we climb

by Phil Bartlett

This was it – the bear meat; and now that many years have passed, I regret that I ate so little of it, for nothing has had, even distantly, the taste of that meat, which is the taste of being strong and free, free also to make mistakes and to be master of one's own destiny.
Primo Levi

 THE ERNEST PRESS

Published by The Ernest Press 1993
© Phil Bartlett

ISBN 0 948153 24 5

British Library Cataloguing-in-Publication Data
A catalogue record for this book is available from
the British Library

Photoset by Parker Typesetting Service, Leicester
Printed by St Edmundsbury Press

Contents

Preface

This book is an attempt to celebrate the nature of mountaineering. My approach is partly scholarly and historical, but it is also unashamedly personal and romantic, and that inevitably leads to some difficult conflicts, of which not the least is the juxtaposition of fact and opinion. Where the conflicts seemed irreconcilable I have, I hope, come down on the side of feeling, on the importance of the *idea*. Thus many of the pen-portraits of historical figures have been written to illustrate a point, and are not intended as complete biographical sketches.

In researching the book I have used many written sources, but the primary source has remained my own experience of climbing, walking and exploration. The result is not an objective assessment of other people's experiences – clearly impossible – but an attempt to convey my own.

But those experiences have been crucially moulded by all those with whom I have shared days on the hill, so it is an enormous pleasure – the greatest pleasure in writing the book – to be able to thank them, and everyone else who has helped. I say very little about friendship in what follows; but companionship, whether it engenders love or hate, is one of mountaineering's strongest experiences. I would also like to thank everyone who has offered advice; I have invariably found it useful, even when I haven't taken it.

I would like to thank Colin Wilson, the late Robert Westall and Livia Gollancz for early encouragement. More recently, Stephen Venables has been very supportive. Most of all, in general terms, I would like to thank Jim Perrin, who has been unstinting in his time and interest, and Lilias Alison, who has proof-read the entire text and made several valuable suggestions.

I have received invaluable help with the collation of photographs, and am most grateful to the following: Mrs Sally Amos; Mrs Rosemary Ballard; Gary Baum; John Beatty; Chris Bonington; Mrs Jennifer Bourdillon; Paul Braithwaite; Elaine Brook; Rab Carrington; John Cleare; Kurt Diemberger; Pat Ewen; Rob Ferguson; Hamish Fulton; Richard Gibbens; Dennis Gray; Lindsay Griffin; Maurice Herzog; John Hunt; John Lagoe; Dave Matthews; Fosco Maraini; Ben Osborne; Paul Nunn; Jim Perrin; Bruce Reid; Dick Renshaw; Simon Richardson; Doug Scott; Sean Smith; Dermot Somers; Jack Soper; David Stewart-Smith; Stephen Venables; Dave Wilkinson; Ken Wilson; Mrs Phyllis Wint. Particularly warm thanks are due to John Cleare, who put a considerable portfolio of work at my disposal.

Many of the early photographs are from the archives of *The Alpine Club*. I would like to thank the President and Committee of the Club, the Assistant Secretary, Sheila Harrison, and Bob Lawford for unending help and patience whilst I rifled through the Club's collections. I would also like to thank Nicky Sherriff of the Royal Geographical

Society, and the staff of the Abbot Hall Gallery, Kendal.

For various points of information and other assistance I would like to thank Marion Power, Sheila Harrison, Audrey Salkeld and Ken Wilson. I have attempted to contact all holders of copyright material and thanks are due to all authors and publishers of books discussed. My sincere apologies to anyone whom I have inadvertently overlooked.

I am very grateful, to say no more, to my publishers, Peter Hodgkiss and Jack Baines, for their faith and support. I want to thank Peter in particular for making many suggestions and saving me from a number of historical blunders.

Finally, I would like to thank my parents, who refound many of the references which I had been inefficient enough to lose. My mother undertook most of the research in London on the early photographs. Without her help the project would never have been finished.

It is to my parents, with love and respect, that I dedicate the book.

1 On the Big Hill

What is the attraction of hills and mountains, 'those prodigious lumps of stone', and why should we want to climb them? These are old questions, and it has become fashionable to regard them as unanswerable, or at least so complex – beauty, excitement, exercise, solitude and companionship are among the obvious answers, and all have some truth – that asking them becomes tantamount to asking why we do anything. By saying everything, you say nothing.

But I believe this is mistaken and that it *is* possible to define their attraction, to find not a single motive but a single underlying source of contentment which remains unchanged and unchangeable, is the same today as it was for the Victorian alpinists, and which connects Himalayan exploration with hill-walking in Britain. It is a source which in the end nurtures and sustains all mountaineering's joys.

Nature has provided us with a variety of excrescences, from the hills of England to the 8000 metre peaks of the Himalaya. *Mountaineering simply means our efforts to get up them under our own steam.* Skis, crampons and ropes are allowed; helicopters are not. Mountaineering is thus an entirely artificial undertaking, the creation of difficulty for its own sake, and at its simplest we climb because we need something to do. At the same time the love of mountains has profound roots; more profound, perhaps, than those of any other sport or pastime. Wherever nature has raised a bump above the plain, it has meant something. Wherever migrating peoples have crossed high passes they have left signs there, flags streaming in the wind. Today we often long for a return to the primitive and a greater simplicity in living, and mountaineering answers that longing powerfully.*

So an unusual breadth of experience is involved, and though this poses problems for the would-be philosopher it is also, I believe, the key. Mountains have the power to involve us totally; 'all human life is there', as someone once said; mountains are symbols not only of aspiration and courage but of something much more complete. That, at least, is the argument of this book.

Mountaineering embraces a broad canvas and includes walking, camping and rock gymnastics as well as the climbing of high snow-covered peaks. Between these activities there is no easy division but a great deal of common ground. Today there are the

---

*As used in this book, 'primitive' and 'primitivism' are not derogatory terms. On the contrary, though it implies a greater simplicity of the physical life, primitivism may involve a mental life of the greatest sophistication – *but a sophistication different from our own.* This was true, for example, of certain social strata in 'Old' Tibet (roughly, Tibet prior to invasion by the Chinese in 1950 and, more recently, by mass tourism). Primitive peoples may or may not be visionaries, but they are invariably less cluttered, both materially and mentally, than ourselves.

'scramblers', fell-walkers who find the well-trodden paths too tame and like to tackle some easy rock route to the top of a Welsh or Cumbrian hill. Two hundred years ago Wordsworth, who epitomised everything we would associate with the best of walking – rhythm, a love of nature, a delight in scenery – produced in *The Prelude* an outstanding poetic expression of the experience of rock-climbing, and Coleridge wrote a timeless description of descending Broad Stand, a short awkward rock-climb which stands across the walker's path between Scafell and Scafell Pike in the English Lake District. He got himself into a 'tremble' about half way down, but made it to safety in the end and walked home in a state of 'almost prophetic trance and delight', aware of a rare 'depth of pleasurable impression' resulting from his 'stretched and anxious' state of mind. None of this has changed. Climbers may be fools, but at their best they are wise fools, able to appreciate anew the pleasures of what that grand old Quaker and Everest climber of the 1920s, Howard Somervell, termed 'the gentler illumination'.

If hard climbing is for the ambitious, walking is for the reflective, and if that suggests a certain pecking order, and that technical aspects are secondary, no more than a means to an end – well, that has always been the traditional view. Jerry Wright, one of the first mountain guides in Britain and a key figure in outdoor education between 1945 and the end of the '60s, believed that 'the quintessence of rock-climbing is to be found in its combination with mountain walking', and Wilfrid Noyce, amongst the best-known and most talented British mountaineers of the immediate pre-war generation, felt that a day's rock-climbing should always be completed by walking to the top of the nearest hill. Apparently he once suggested this after climbing with that master of bluntness and pith, Don Whillans. Whillans' reply, alas, has not been preserved.

But although in spirit this book is as much about Sunday fell-walking as it is about climbing mountains in the greater ranges, in terms of literary sources it is climbing and exploration, and particularly climbing and exploration in the Alps and the Himalaya, which must form its core. Most walkers are operating far from the limit of their abilities, and although Somervell's 'gentler illumination' may be an illumination of the most affecting and valuable kind, the very fact that it is gentle makes it terribly difficult to know what to say. The extreme climber can at least abandon the rules of English prose and invent an extreme literary style to suit his experience, but the nature of walking seems to preclude this, and its followers are forever trying to follow in the footsteps of the romantic poets.

It is the big hill which offers both the most wide-ranging and the most intense experiences, and it is precisely this combination in mountaineering which has produced the best – and the worst – literature. Intense experiences produce dilemmas, and it is dilemmas more than any other single factor which underlie what mountaineers have to say.

2   Ranges Beyond and Yet Beyond . . .

The attraction of mountains is that they offer a new perspective on life, a refreshed sense of its vitality and exhilaration. In the ordinary way life becomes rather drab, so we look for ways to make it less so, and mountaineering offers itself as a possible solution; we remember those days of wide horizons and tired limbs, with the sun flashing on the snow or swirling clouds threatening to engulf us. We feel at once excited, uplifted, refreshed.

The whole object of the exercise is to capture those rare moments 'either on the mountains, or perhaps in some distant view of them, when life and joy have assumed new meanings, and the world's horizons suddenly broken down and shown us realms of dream beyond and yet beyond'. Dr Raymond Greene, who was on Kamet and Everest in the 1930s, called his autobiography *Moments of Being*, and in so doing summed up the object of mountaineering very neatly. His brother, the novelist Graham Greene, had as a boy played Russian Roulette; he would take a revolver onto Berkhamstead heath, insert one bullet, spin the chambers and fire at his head. When there was only a click he felt a fantastic exhilaration and freedom – life contained 'an infinite number of possibilities'. There is a degree of common ground between the two brothers' experiences, yet it is impossible not to believe that Raymond had found the healthier and altogether superior route of the two.

In 1934 an unknown Englishman with no climbing experience, Maurice Wilson, set out to solo Mt Everest. He began by flying single-handed from England to Asia despite no previous flying experience and every sort of official discouragement. Having arrived in India, he hired Sherpas and set off on a clandestine trek through Tibet to the north side of the mountain, where he somehow succeeded in getting up the difficult Rongbuk Glacier to below the north face. There he died, alone in his tent, of cold and exhaustion. It was a forlorn outcome to absurdly optimistic hopes, yet when members of Eric Shipton's Everest reconnaissance expedition found Wilson's body the following year, they did so with a sense of respect. Wilson had not had a clue what he was doing, but at least he had *tried*. If it was irresponsible, it was also rather glorious. Wilson kept a diary in his last days, and besides recording his privations and futile hopes for the summit, he wrote something which all mountaineers will immediately understand and respect: 'I have the distinct feeling that I've at least had some kick out of life'.

These moments of intense life take many forms. Sometimes they are flashes of sheer exhilaration and nothing else; pure sensation, almost sensuality, with no mental content, no moralising or philosophising, nothing but the moment. At others their character is altogether quieter and such as to encourage reflection, perhaps suggesting new ideas about life and what it means, about our place in the world and how we should live. In

'. . . realms of dream beyond and yet beyond.' En route to the Lemonsbjerge and the East Greenland coast in 1

...th the joys of exploration and the feeling of another era filling my mind. *(Photo: David Stewart-Smith.)*

Francis William Bourdillon (1852–1921), whose 'moments' remain the goal of every generation, and Eduardo Defargo (left), proprietor of the Hotel Beau Sejour, Champery, where Bourdillon habitually stayed, on the summit of the Matterhorn, 8.30 a.m., 27th July, 1908. Whilst still at university Bourdillon assured himself of literary immortality with the following lines:

> The night has a thousand eyes,
>   And the day but one;
> Yet the light of the bright world dies,
>   With the dying sun.
>
> The mind has a thousand eyes,
>   And the heart but one;
> Yet the light of a whole life dies,
>   When love is done.

He became a tutor to various aristocratic families until a comfortable marriage gave him the means to devote himself exclusively to various – mainly scholarly – interests.
(Photo: courtesy of the late J. F. Bourdillon FRCS.)

these cases they may be truly visionary. But whatever the form, whether pure sensation or philosophically suggestive, they make life seem desirable, valuable, 'real', in a way which much of the time it does not.

In *Summits and Secrets*, one of the best of the modern climbing autobiographies, the Austrian mountaineer Kurt Diemberger devotes a chapter to crystal-hunting in the European Alps, at first sight an odd thing to do in a climbing book. But this section is in fact of central importance, for the crystal is representative of that childish wonder and ecstasy which Diemberger is to spend so much of his adult life trying to regain. Precious and semi-precious stones are not only status symbols and convertible currency; in many ages, if not our own, they have been valued as representative of the visionary state, intense, concentrated, utterly clear. Diemberger searches for crystals on Alpine mountainsides where they flash in the torchlight, rare and precious against the darkness. This is a metaphor for man's struggle to *see*, and the crystals, symbols of his infrequent success.

Moments of insight, those moments which bring a feeling of 'Ah, so *this* is living!' are the high points of mountain experience, and I believe that, in their attempts to achieve them, mountaineers are making use of two fundamental characteristics of the human condition.

Noyce found a good word for one of them; expansionism. Something of what expansionism means is to be found in J.R.L. Anderson's book *The Ulysses Factor*. Anderson is trying to answer that perennial question: what is it that motivates people to exploration and physical adventure, whether on land, sea or in the air? The simplest answer is that it is the hope of gain, either of goods, land, political influence or fame. But it has always been clear that our adventurous instincts are really much more complex than this and that there is something more subtle involved. Early explorers may have had commercial motives or been lured on by fame. These attractions remain today. But underneath them is something more private – more private yet almost universal, something which Anderson defines as an innate urge to discover for its own sake, a pure curiosity which has no utilitarian purpose yet is deep and insistent. He sees Homer's hero as the type-figure, and quotes Tennyson's poem:

> I cannot rest from travel: I will drink
> Life to the lees:

the last lines of which have come to be closely associated in mountaineers' minds with the explorer Eric Shipton:

> . . . all experience is an arch wherethro'
> Gleams that untravelled world, whose margin fades
> For ever and for ever when I move.

Whether Ulysses is a real historical figure is irrelevant. His importance is as a myth, an image of the urge to explore the physical environment and extend horizons.

In *The Springs of Adventure* Noyce hints at a rather wider conception, something which recognises not only physical urges but humanity's wish for *mental* expansion. Noyce was a mountaineer, Anderson a sailor, but neither saw any essential difference between mountaineers, sailors, the pioneers of early aviation, or arctic explorers. Why do they do it – any of them? Having devoted most of his book to listing the standard answers, Noyce admits that he has probably missed the essence of it. Then he suddenly becomes interesting; 'In pride of our humanity . . . we go for the new and so add, or endeavour to add, cubits to our stature', he writes. 'It is not always pleasant, but it is very human'. He goes on to relate a dream in which he sees a man, and towering over him, a mountain. The man is determined to reach and surpass the mountain, and swells himself up so that he grows until he can see over the rocks and vegetation around him. Then he bursts. 'The sequel was unexpected. Inside that man, as it seemed, was another man, unless he were the soul of the first. He was larger than the original; as if that experience of growing remained with him and allowed him to keep something of his new stature. Moreover his eyes were curiously bright, and I thought that from over those first little ridges and shrubs he must have been able to see new country, which it was a delight to remember even now.'

That is a powerful image, all the more interesting for being an unconscious invention, and its primary significance comes from a non-literal interpretation. After all, the purely physical aspects of adventure are beginning to look rather pointless. Most corners of the globe have been explored, and improvements in equipment are fast rendering almost anything possible. In these circumstances it is natural that human curiosity should increasingly become a mental curiosity. And when that curiosity is turned in on ourselves, even ostensibly 'outward' pursuits, such as mountaineering or ocean sailing, can take on an inward significance with psychological, even religious, repercussions.

In his classic *The Savage and Beautiful Country* the psychiatrist Alan McGlashan sees man as a player in an evolutionary drama in which all life is struggling to expand. Even space exploration is a part of this; '. . . the acorn falling softly to the forest floor, the sycamore seed equipped with tiny helicopter wings to further its flight from the parent tree, the horse-chestnut capsule pronged and spiked like any sputnik . . . I suggest that the manned space-ship is only the latest of an almost infinite series of such attempts; the ceaseless, compulsive efforts of Life to propagate itself, to survive somehow, somewhere, to find new lodgements and new possibilities of growth . . .' The situation cannot be avoided; we have no more choice about exploring space than the sycamore seed has in flying from its parent.

McGlashan makes a distinction between physical conquest and mental conquest, particularly when discussing what, from the human point of view, is the most important adventure of all, the struggle to conquer time. The physical conquest of time is something relatively new in human experience, beginning with the smith, from whom we have learnt to transform the very substances of the earth, and at rates far exceeding those which geological time would dictate. Its future, in time travel or other sci-fi fantasies, we can only guess at. The mental conquest, on the other hand, is as old as time, and the archaic methods of how to achieve it, centring round the notion of sacrament and the experience of religious ritual, have never been bettered. They are the experiences of primitive peoples, for whom physical processes are fixed, part of the essential rhythm of things, and therefore not to be tampered with.

But to suggest that mountaineering is just another example of human curiosity and the urge to explore would clearly be unsatisfactory. The existence of these feelings is not in doubt – but why mountains? Why the pain, the danger, the effort, that mountaineering involves?

Part of the answer is that mountaineering takes us to the frontier personally. In mountains we experience the new in the most direct way; there is nothing second-hand about struggling for one's life in a mountain storm or seeing the sun rise over the lip of the world from a high camp. Many forms of expansionism cannot offer this. It is curiosity which leads the human race to seek explicit knowledge, 'facts', and to construct scientific truth, and without it many new achievements (and space exploration is as good as example as any) would be quite impossible. But scientific truth is impersonal knowledge and this is not what interests mountaineers. The expansionism which motivates people to climb mountains and which exhilarates them is always concerned primarily with personal sensations and, to put it more generally, with personal knowledge. It is not concerned with 'progress', or indeed with impersonal knowledge at all.

To anyone with a knowledge of mountaineering history this may seem a dubious claim. During the nineteenth and early part of the twentieth centuries, mountaineering was often justified by appealing to its impersonal aspects. Both explorers and technical climbers played down anything which smacked of egocentricity and claimed for mountaineering a series of socially useful functions ranging from glory of the Empire to economic or military advantage. Everest climbers spoke of the vicarious adventure they provided for ordinary people at home and of the example of team-spirit and selflessness which they set. Indeed, this attitude was evident as recently as John Hunt's successful expedition in 1953. But one wonders whether these views were not as much a reflection of what was then socially acceptable and politically shrewd as what was true. The literature as a whole seems to leave little doubt that mountaineering is, and always has been, a personal matter. And it is their admirable determination to make this clear and avoid cant at all costs which has led some modern writers, living as they do in a more candid age, to swing the pendulum too far from the earlier idealism and deny not only impersonal motives but even the existence of friendship and camaraderie in mountaineering. This is quite a different thing from extolling the primacy of personal motives, and in my experience, quite wrong. It encourages too simplistic a view of the game – that achievement is all, and someone else to tie the rope to simply a regrettable necessity. The truth, surely, is this: mountaineering is selfish, but it can also be the source of the most glorious of friendships, and a time to experience real human closeness.

One of the most quoted of the 'impersonal' factors has been science. Many of the alpine pioneers of the eighteenth and nineteenth centuries thought science central, and there is no better example than the Frenchman Horace Benedict de Saussure, the instigator of the first ascent of Mont Blanc. De Saussure first came to Chamonix in 1760, at the age of twenty, and immediately offered a reward to the first person to get to the top. His interest was not as a mountaineer (if it had been, he would never have offered such a reward; he would have tried to get there first himself) but as a scientist, and when he made the second ascent in 1787 it was strictly in the cause of science:

> My object was not only to reach the highest point, I was bound to make the scientific observations and experiments which alone gave value to my venture.

More to the point, he meant it.

The British mountaineer John Tyndall, who produced a number of works on the movement of glaciers in the 1850s, is another example. In due course Tyndall became involved in a celebrated argument about the importance of science with another of the Victorian era's leading figures, Leslie Stephen. Stephen disparaged science as an irrelevant sideline; Tyndall was enraged. Even today the interplay between mountaineering and science has not wholly disappeared. The English *Alpine Journal*, for example, still carries its original subtitle: 'A record of mountain adventure and scientific observation'.

But none of this means that science is fundamental to mountaineering. It is simply a reminder that scientific investigation can be practised in mountains as well as anywhere else, that it has developed mountain specialisms, and that in Alpinism's formative years a belief in science and its benefits was running through society with much more certainty than it does today. Any new environment promises fresh scientific discoveries and, in the nineteenth century, mountains held out that promise. No-one knew much about the effects of altitude or the movement of glaciers but they wanted to know, so scientists had, of necessity, to become climbers. They took all sorts of apparatus with them to the summits, laboriously boiling water and recording temperatures, measuring wind speeds and finding each other's pulse rates. They took it very seriously, and if in looking back it all seems rather comical it is because we now know the answers. Where we don't know, we continue to take our mountain science as seriously as the pioneers ever did. The obvious example is mountain medicine.

Today, when many mountaineers have no interest in science at all, it seems unnecessary to say that the mountaineering passion can stand on its own feet, without the 'excuse' of science. But I think this was true even in the pioneering days of the eighteenth and nineteenth centuries. The *raison d'être* of mountaineering comes from the nature of man,

The view first seen by Michel-Gabriel Paccard and Jacques Balmat, and *not* by de Saussure; the view north-eastwards from the summit of Mont Blanc with France on the left, Italy on the right, and the peaks of the *Valais*, Switzerland, in the distance.
(Photo: John Cleare.)

not from the character or interests of an age. Tyndall and other climber/scientists simply had a dual motivation. One was science; the other was the 'pure' motive of mountaineering for its own sake.

Even the scientists who start off dry and single-minded usually get caught by the mountains' enchantment in the end. De Saussure certainly did. His upbringing was as a scientist and he went into the mountains with science in mind. Yet his interest in the Alps and their inhabitants went far beyond a purely scientific curiosity. Though he fought like all good scientists against 'alpine mysticism', those vague religious notions which mountains are so good at encouraging, he was affected by them more than he cared to admit. In due course he let his guard slip and gave expression to a mountaineer's jealousy, writing of Dr Paccard, who with Jacques Balmat made the first ascent of Mont Blanc and thus won the reward he had offered:

> He seems to have taken pains everywhere to have gone a little further and a little higher than I have been.

But if dual motives are common they are also confusing. The early attempts to climb Everest brought forth both the scientific and the private forms of curiosity; on the one hand can it physically be done, and if so is bottled oxygen necessary; on the other, can *I* do it, and if so what is the sensation at this frontier? These motives got hopelessly mixed, leading to endless doubts about the purpose of it all. George Mallory felt that it sometimes seemed 'more like war than mountaineering', and his colleague Tom Longstaff just wanted it all to be over, so that he could turn with an easy conscience to 'the true enjoyment of the Himalaya, most likely to be found at about 20,000 ft or less'. The never-ending disagreements between the supporters of large expeditions and those who preferred shoe-string efforts were a reflection of the confusion. Was the most important thing to reach the top at all costs, or did the way it was done matter? Which was more important: the ultimate success of an expedition, or the personal satisfaction of its members on the way? And was it right to be diverting some of the effort which could be used to climb the mountain on to scientific projects?

Even mountain exploration, which is relatively easy to justify in concrete terms, has never been driven purely by science and the pursuit of 'facts'. Though there have certainly been explorers who have penetrated mountain country for purely practical purposes, hated every minute of it, and put up with it simply for the sake of the results, there have been many others who, whilst making important additions to diplomacy, warmongering or geography, have loved exploration purely and simply for itself. And all the explorers we recognise as being in the mainstream of mountaineering history – Tom Longstaff, Eric Shipton, Bill Tilman, for example – were of this kind. They had a very personal relationship to what they did. This also seems to have been true of some of the Pundits, those extraordinary servants of British India sent clandestinely into Tibet to map unknown territory at a time when the British themselves could not gain access. In the latter half of the nineteenth century men like Nain Singh Rawat, Kishen Singh and

'The Pundits, as well as the gentlemen explorers, were motivated by something deeper.' Kishen Singh, one of the greatest of the Pundits, on his doorstep at Tejam, Almora District, India, in 1907. *(Photo of Kishen Singh by E.J. Mardon courtesy of the Royal Geographical Society.)*

Right: Charles Warren, Peter Lloyd, Bill Tilman, Peter Oliver, Frank Smythe, Noel Odell and Eric Shipton on the 1938 Everest expedition. Under Tilman's leadership the expedition style was, inevitably, lightweight. This extended even to food – ultimately a more emotive subject on expeditions than oxygen sets, number of Sherpas or other ethical niceties. Tilman's characteristically spartan rations were strongly criticised by, for example, Warren and Odell.

Sarat Chandra Das achieved some extraordinary journeys, variously disguised as Beshahri horse-dealers, Ladakhi pilgrims or Chinese monks. They measured distances by surreptitiously counting paces and recorded their findings in secret code concealed in portable Tibetan prayer wheels. The Pundits are amongst the true heroes of mountain exploration, showing more devotion to the task than can ever be explained purely on the basis of professional pride or fear of their superiors. The Pundits, as well as the gentlemen explorers, were motivated by something deeper.

Mountaineers have often been deliberately misleading about their motives. In *Four Fallacies* (*Mountain 82*, 1981), Peter Donnelly has argued that four of the commonest claims made for climbing, that it is not competitive or fundamentally dangerous, that it is character-building and that it leads people to form close friendships, are in fact all fallacies. So why do they survive? Donnelly suggests two reasons. The first is that they are encouraged by the outdoor education movement. Climbing – outdoor education in general – can justify its place in modern education if it is believed to be character-building, but if it is seen to be overtly competitive it is liable to be disapproved of by large sections of the educational lobby and, if dangerous, by parents.

Secondly, climbers want above all else to be left alone, and this is more likely to happen if they are perceived by the rest of society as being reliable and responsible. And this means downplaying things like competition and risk. One is reminded of the Matterhorn accident of 1865 and the crisis in the public image of climbing which resulted. Edward Whymper had finally climbed the mountain but in the process four men, including one paid employee, had died. *The Times* was highly critical: 'What is he doing there, and what right has he to throw away the gift of life . . .? Is it common-sense? Is it allowable? Is it not wrong?' Some years later, when alpine accidents were again in the headlines, Queen Victoria also wished to interfere. Disraeli dissuaded her.

Looking back, the nineteenth century pioneers were probably safe from significant interference, not least because most came from the upper echelons of society. But similar attacks on mountaineering have been occurring ever since and, as a result, competition and risk have had to be downplayed in favour of other factors. Character-building and friendship are two of them, and perhaps science is another. Science can hardly be regarded as selfish, and, above all, science as a motive is understandable. Because scientific expeditions have an easily understood and approved motive they are less likely to be regarded with political suspicion than purely 'sporting' ventures. A foreigner wanting to come to our country to *climb*? Surely not; he must be up to no good! All in all, taking science on board can be useful. Bill Tilman is a classic example of someone who felt mountaineering to be entirely worthwhile and justifiable on its own terms, yet when in 1949 the Nepalese authorities decided that they would let his expedition into their country only on condition it included a scientific element, he bent with the wind. He was the first Westerner to be given such an opportunity for many years and he wasn't going to throw it away. 'To be too stiff in opinion is a grave fault' he wrote philosophically. 'A man should be sure of more than his principles before deciding never to break them.'

But the argument can be taken further because knowledge, or 'facts', far from being a help to someone seeking new sensations, may prove a positive hindrance. And so arises that deep ambivalence towards information of all kinds which is fundamental to mountaineering.

One obviously needs a certain amount of information to get to one's mountain, and a professed interest in gathering more attracts sponsorship. Yet at the same time information is deeply alien, because *it enables imagination to usurp the actual experiencing of the frontier.* Imagination is the enemy of mountaineering, because the mountaineer who is over-sensitive, over-imaginative, will be able to visualise it all and there will then be no reason to actually 'do'. Mountaineers derive an intense sense of life from exploring the unknown, but to deliver the goods it must be really unknown, and that means something which one's imagination cannot construct for itself. If imagination can construct it, what possible point can there be in physically going there? Armchair mountaineering will do just as well. The result is a deep antagonism between the mountaineering ethic (which is about doing), and imagination; and there is a real need, if one is to retain one's enthusiasm, to keep imagination in check.

This state of affairs is not, of course, a very favourable reflection on mountaineering or those who practise it, and it has often been agonised over by the sport's more reflective devotees. In recent times the English mountaineer Peter Boardman is an outstanding example. The Scotsman Dougal Haston is another. Haston once remarked that he often turned back on easier routes because they were not sufficiently testing. His implication, surely, was that he could see the future too clearly for there to be any point. Imagination spoilt everything.

The situation was essentially no different a hundred years ago when the Englishman Alfred Frederick Mummery was pushing forward standards in the Alps. Mummery was to write in *My Climbs in the Alps and Caucasus*, one of the great books of nineteenth century mountaineering, of just how boring he found the ordinary route up Mont Blanc. Why? Because the climb was well known and Mummery was experienced. The result was that all the way up his imagination could paint a detailed picture of just what was going to happen next. Mummery climbed not for the view but for the rewards of the unknown – one of the reasons he is widely regarded as one of the fathers of modern mountaineering – so it is hardly surprising that 'revolutionary ideas quickly gained possession of the party, and culminated in the absolute refusal of its amateur members to go another step. Despite the indignation and scorn of the professionals, we tumbled and glissaded back to the Grand Mulets, picked up our few belongings and ran down to the Pierre Pointue and Chamonix'.

A later pioneer, Geoffrey Winthrop Young, wrote that we return to the hills to be reminded of what we have forgotten, and that is true. But first we have to be convinced that we have forgotten something and that returning is worth the effort. The effect of information is both to convince us that yes, there really is a more rewarding world out

Walking at Wasdale Head in the English Lake District, where the scenery is as marvellous as ever but a sense of mystery and awe is not so easily achieved. *(Photo: Peter Hodgkiss.)*

there, but at the same time to make us doubt. Given television and other people's accounts, one is fooled – and oh, so easily! – into believing that armchair mountaineering is as good as the real thing.

And there is a corollary to all this. Just as too fertile an imagination is a problem, so a straightforward knowledge of what one wants to do without agonising overmuch about why, is for mountaineers a distinct advantage. In our own time Chris Bonington has demonstrated conclusively how the excitement which comes from exploring the unknown, when coupled with a fundamentally cheerful temperament, can support an enviably boyish enthusiasm about life right through middle age.

It is the would-be explorer who feels the information dilemma most acutely. The climber/gymnast at least has the technical interest of his chosen route to enjoy even if the mountains have been stripped of their mysteries, but for the explorer the mystery is absolutely crucial. Though at first sight exploration is about concrete information and explicit achievement – to be the first to penetrate that far range, the first to bring back the gold hidden within the blank on the map – this is not the real motivation. The essence of the art, and it is an art, is almost the complete opposite: living in the present, the appreciation of the moment. Longstaff argued that people are always putting off 'real living' to some future, and so our whole existence becomes geared to tomorrow. We do not live in the present moment, and one of the reasons we do not is that information and imagination are able to transfer the centre of things into the future. Without them we would be doing what we should be doing: living in 'now'. The life of the explorer is rewarding because imagination suddenly finds itself powerless.

Nevertheless, something of the explorer's unhappiness colours all mountaineering and even today's fell-walkers might feel a tinge of regret. The sale of guide-books is enormous, but many of us have a love/hate relationship with the things. The guide-book is useful; at the same time it is 'a bastard creature, a detestable hybrid of snow and rock mixed up with paper'. Apart from becoming more crowded, the hills lose their mystery. Thus one of the deepest joys is lost, and walking is reduced to little more than healthy exercise and a pleasant view. A similar situation exists in rock-climbing. Everyone wants information, and yet . . . and yet the hope that somehow it will all go away lingers on, sometimes in perverse obscurantism, replacing information by disinformation, sometimes in bold attempts to create no-information areas where everyone will agree to climb but not to publish.

The ambivalence is profound. It has always existed and it remains as unsolvable as ever. In *The Mountain Men*, an account of the early history of Welsh rock-climbing, Alan Hankinson recalls the heated debate which raged over the question of publication nearly a century ago when the photographers George and Ashley Abraham produced one of the first rock-climbing guidebooks, *Rock-Climbing in North Wales*. Their book did not meet with universal approval. Commenting on the controversy, Hankinson remarks that he thinks it strange, with the benefit of hindsight, that such questions should have aroused such passions as they did. After all, mountains and mountaineering now form a small but established part of the publishing business.

But this is to miss the point entirely. It suggests that the controversy has been solved to people's satisfaction, but I do not think it has, and I doubt it ever will be. Publishing has certainly 'happened', and there has been an explosion of information, but I suspect that in the heart of most mountaineers it is as worrying an issue today as it ever was. No doubt some of those who criticised the Abrahams were simply jealous, and some were certainly socially prejudiced; the Abrahams were tradesmen, making a good living out of climbing at a time when much of the climbing establishment thought this quite improper. But others had seen the real seriousness of the problem. Hankinson thinks that all the hand-wringing must have seemed 'slightly odd even at the time, for many of the early climbers had been attracted to the sport by reading the books of Whymper and Leslie Stephen and Mummery. Almost without exception, they were members of the Climbers' Club, or the Alpine Club or both, and both clubs issued regular journals'. But far from dismissing it, this merely underlines the depth of the dilemma. It is perfectly possible to have conflicting feelings, all of which are genuine, particularly in an activity as contrived as mountaineering. 'Do I contradict myself? / Very well then, I contradict myself, / (I am large, I contain multitudes)' as Whitman has it. As total information becomes ever more total, one cannot simply divide people into a group that wants it and a group that prefers ignorance. Most sincerely want both.

The essence of mountaineering is to touch frontiers and the edge of experience. It is not holding back; it is pushing forward, pushing oneself forward. To call this selfish is to suggest a moral judgement, but it is certainly egocentric, which is what the Italian mountaineer Walter Bonatti was getting at when he called mountaineering an 'affirmation of personality'. The mountaineer stands out as unusual, as life in a wild and largely dead world, and if phrases such as 'conquering the summit' are no longer quite the fashionable thing to say, they nevertheless betray the true psychological effect. One affirms one's will, one's ability to do, and thus gains a stronger sense of self.

One may even discover what that sense of self really is. It is common for mountaineers, and particularly those who operate at a high level, to explain their pursuit as an investigation of the self or a testing ground in which one discovers one's strengths and weaknesses. In *Changabang* Doug Scott tells us that 'the more one goes into mountains the more one realises they are but a medium for exploration into oneself'. 'But what could be more reasonable than finding out about yourself?' asks Haston, expressing the same outlook. The French mountaineer Pierre Mazeaud called his autobiography *Naked Before the Mountain*, and a similar strain of romanticism colours all Bonatti's writings.

But if mountains are an arena in which we find out about ourselves, the findings are revealed to others too, so they can put friendships under great strain. Some expedition books seem to be little more than sagas of broken friendships and painful self-revelation, which can be tedious, but they express an important aspect of mountaineering nonetheless, and are probably less misleading than claims that it is character-building or creates deep friendships. Rather, the mountains look on impassively as our actions merely demonstrate with a new clarity what is already there.

This comes out in a passage Bonington wrote in the 1960s. He has abandoned first a commission in the army and then the life of a business executive, and at last launched out as a freelance climber and writer. Life is not easy. He is acutely aware that he is spending most of his time giving the same old boring lecture about yesterday's climb (the north face of the Eiger), and doing no more climbing than many of his friends with regular jobs. He has a young family, feels financially insecure, and approaches the New Year with a sense of increasing depression and worry about the future. Is it all a terrible mistake?

But it takes only one day of glorious winter sunshine and climbing in Scotland to change his mood and restore his confidence. At the top of Crowberry Gully in Glencoe on New Year's day:

> I knew a delicious sense of achievement – of freedom – of pure, simple joy at my situation; how different from the dark mood of the previous night. Climbing, the great healer, had restored my self-confidence.

Also, one feels, his certainty that this was what he wanted to do.

To go where no-one has gone before and do what no-one else has done is the most obvious and perhaps the most attractive way to affirm one's sense of self. It is heroic, and it is certainly romantic; crudely speaking, the criterion of romantic success is to create a world different from anyone else's. Climbers, walkers and explorers are all drawn to tread new ground, and the heightened awareness which new places and dangerous situations bring to human consciousness is paralleled by an equally new sense of personal importance, of 'What, me? here?'

'On the first of the new rock climbs which I made in North Wales ... I looked down the grey falls of scree on to the wide green Nant Francon valley with its thin riband of winding road, and I thrilled suddenly with a new feeling', writes Winthrop Young. 'For hundreds and thousands of years, high and close above the passing and repassing of countless generations, this upright corner of beautiful and soiled England – or rather Wales – had been waiting unvisited, untrodden, even unseen, until, during the few days of my own short life, the climbing enthusiasm had broken over us, and had set me, miraculously, upon it. Here upon this ledge since earth took form out of chaos no one before me had set foot. On that glister of crystal quartz under my hand no eye before mine had ever rested.'

To feel that is tremendously exhilarating, and it is not a purely competitive exhilaration. The essence is more subtle, being an affirmation of self in the face of the physical world as much as in the face of other people. However, it can only be experienced in uncharted territory or in places which appear to be uncharted, or, at the very least, in places which are empty. And this is worrying. Genuine blanks on the map are in increasingly short supply and must soon run out altogether, and whilst the existence of pristine territory which *seems* to be uncharted is something which in theory might be kept going for ever – such places would enable one to practise 'pseudo-exploration', not quite the real thing but pretty close to it – there are few signs of there being any real will to put this theory into practice.

If I visit an area which has been explored yet I am unaware of it, is my experience any less satisfying than 'genuine' exploration? If I leave the guidebook behind and see no trace of human beings does it really matter if other people have been there before me? If my ignorance is total, then surely not. The trouble is, ignorance rarely is total. If one goes to any high valley in the Alps today and sees no sign of human activity, it will still be impossible to believe that no-one else has been there. Simple common sense dictates that one cannot be the first. The result is that the total exploratory experience is today impossible anywhere in the Alps and in due course will become impossible everywhere else too.

Admittedly this only removes a small part of what exploration has to offer, and it is the only part which it is impossible to preserve. The rest *could* be preserved if we were to pursue a deliberate limiting of information and an almost obsessive care in leaving the land unaltered by our passing. But the practical difficulties of this, whether on British hills or on the Everest trek in Nepal, are too obvious to need repeating here. There are a lot of people around, and it is very difficult for them all to pass without trace. It is assumed that people shouldn't leave litter because it is unsightly and unhealthy, and so it is. But what is not so widely appreciated is that it also makes it impossible for the pseudo-explorer to experience even half decently the ego-affirmation of genuine exploration.

All of which should help us to understand the place competition has in mountaineering and the ease with which it can be misunderstood. The simple situation certainly exists – many people are competitive; some of them like climbing; some like to mix the two together. But this is the less important part of the story. What is more interesting is that people often become competitive only out of a kind of regrettable necessity. It is circumstance, rather than inner human nature, that forces them into it.

Winter climbing in Scotland is a good example. For many years, roughly until the early 1960s, Scottish winter climbing was an esoteric enthusiasm, with only a handful of devotees, and it would be unusual to find anyone else on the same mountain, let alone the same climb. But today its popularity has so increased, and good climbing conditions are so fickle, that people find themselves competing against their will. It is a situation we are all familiar with and it is more than a little absurd: there in some beautiful Scottish corrie which hears nothing but the raven for most of the year, you suddenly realise there are other people; you know beyond any doubt that they are heading for the same climb as yourself; and it ruins it. This is not what anyone came for. The hope was for freedom, ice-blue skies and a feeling of heroism. Instead, something depressingly like the work-a-day world – competition, people, communicating, all those things one goes into the mountains to escape – has found its way even to here. Those who refuse to take part in the race to be first find themselves shivering at the back of a long queue waiting hours to

'The hope was for freedom, ice-blue skies and a feeling of heroism. . . .' Comb Gully Buttress, Ben Nevis, February 1993. On this occasion Gary Baum and I enjoyed the route on a perfect winter's day but 'the Ben' was hardly quiet. When I first climbed it with Lindsay Griffin on a foul day in the mid '70s we had the mountain to ourselves, but Lindsay's legendary reticence as to his experience and ability misled climbers at the CIC memorial hut and we arrived back at our car in the early hours to be greeted by a rescue party. *(Photo: Gary Baum.)*

do a climb which has by then utterly lost its appeal.

The absurdity is underlined by the knowledge that after a week or two of this frantic activity the corrie will return to silence, nothing but the raven and the wind. So why not go then? The problem is that climbers have extremely narrow and specific ideas about which bit of mountain is the interesting bit and they are fussy, with good reason, about the weather they are prepared to tackle it in. The result is that climbs tend to be either totally deserted or impossibly congested.

People want to go for the best, and always have. It is not a problem peculiar to our age. In the 1860s there was still a vast amount of unexplored ground in the European Alps but the Matterhorn seemed to be the best of it and the result was a classic early example of overcrowding and a mountain's ascent being motivated by competition.

Edward Whymper, the organiser and moving force behind the first ascent, wanted to climb the Matterhorn very much; but would he have wanted to if he had been the only person in the world? Somehow one doubts it, and it is this as much as the drama of the climb or the impressiveness of the Matterhorn as a symbol which makes the ascent historically important. For there is no evidence that Whymper was an outstanding climber. He made a number of new climbs, both in the Alps and in South America, but so did almost everybody at that time – there was so much scope. Whymper was in fact no better than many of his contemporaries and without the Matterhorn success and the tragedy of the descent when the least experienced member of the party, Douglas Hadow, slipped and dragged himself and four others to their deaths, his name would be less celebrated.

By the summer of 1865 Whymper had been circling the Matterhorn for years, planning strategies and making attempts. Then he suddenly discovered that his former accomplice Jean Carrel, the adventurous and strong-willed Italian peasant with whom he had made all his early forays on the mountain, was on the point of leading an all-Italian attempt. And that provided the essential impetus:

> The higher we rose, the more intense became the excitement. What if we should be beaten at the last moment? The slope eased off, at length we could be detached, and Croz and I, dashing away, ran a neck-and-neck race, which ended in a dead heat. At 1.40 p.m. the world was at our feet, and the Matterhorn was conquered. Hurrah! Not a footstep could be seen.

That last is a moment of intense reward, seemingly impossible to preserve except by extending the uncertainty itself. The Matterhorn has two summits, one overlooking Switzerland, the other Italy. They are virtually the same height. Whymper, one imagines, had that delicious feeling; he *knew* he had won but had yet to confirm it. He climbed over to the Italian summit and to his relief found no sign of his rivals. Then he saw them far below, climbing slowly upwards. With that final confirmation of victory the party gave full reign to their feelings, Croz and Whymper driving in their alpenstocks and prising away a torrent of stones which poured down on the luckless Italians. Or so we are told; whether any of this actually happened is a moot point. Whymper knew what made for a good story and was not averse to a little poetic licence.

The Matterhorn put Whymper in the public eye and kept him there. This did nothing for his popularity amongst his contemporaries. John Norman Collie, one of the most urbane of the Victorian gentleman mountaineers and a keen explorer of the mountains of western Canada at the end of the century, wrote to a friend:

> I doubt whether you have heard that the great Whymper is about to attack the Rockies during 1901–2–3. He has got the two finest Swiss guides, Klucker and Pollinger, and two others and will go to Banff and then polish off all the peaks . . . He will simply go and gobble up the whole lot.
>
> As a hunting ground for amateurs the country was big enough and to spare, but when a professional team lets itself loose – well all I can say is *damn* the man!

This kind of sentiment has been directed at professional mountaineers many, many times since. It seems quite modern, as does Carrel's fate in missing the boat on the Matterhorn. As the local man, Carrel was confident he would be the first to climb the peak he had known all his life. But the pace was hotting up, and it was no longer possible to keep putting things off until next year.

This had already become apparent during Alfred Wills' ascent of the Wetterhorn eleven years earlier. The Wetterhorn rises above Grindelwald much as the Matterhorn does above Zermatt, and Wills' party, consisting of himself and four guides, found themselves in competition with two unknown Swiss peasants – 'piratical adventurers' Wills called them – one of whom was carrying a fir tree which he intended to set up on the summit. He was Christian Almer, destined to become a brilliant alpine guide and to polish off many of the most important unclimbed peaks in the next twenty years. A local chamois hunter, Almer had heard about Wills' intentions and decided to get there first. After a shouting match the two parties joined forces and in due course planted on the summit both Almer's fir tree and a large metal flag brought up by Wills. Half the team cheered wildly and waved their arms. The other half admonished them for not showing due respect. 'One must never shout on the high peaks,' warned one. 'One never knows what will happen there.'

The shape and interest of these ascents derives very largely from their competitive spice. Things were no different then; nothing changes in our motives, only the way we interpret and write about them; in both stories we recognise ourselves. A few years later, Mummery wrote of the first ascent of one of the most celebrated of Alpine peaks: 'In order to prevent the remainder of the party scrambling up with undue facility and thus exposing the Grepon to scorn, I judiciously urged them not to waste time by sending up the axes and luggage on the rope, but to sling the axes on their arms and distribute the luggage amongst the rest of the party. I found this eminently successful, and a most material aid in impressing my companions with a due respect for the crag'. We might feel that his style of writing is now outmoded, but not the sentiment. And it was not because he was competitive that the mountaineering establishment of the time disliked Mummery; it was because he was honest. Petrarch climbing Mont Ventoux in 1336 would probably have been competitive if there had been anyone there to compete with. Unfortunately his account only tells us that whilst enjoying the view from the summit he opened a copy of Augustine's *Confessions*, alighting on a passage admonishing him for going to admire 'the high places of mountains, the great waves of the sea, the wide currents of rivers, the circuit of the ocean, and the orbits of the stars' and ignoring more proper pursuits. No further climbs by Petrarch are recorded.

But what starts off as competitive success, the stark elation of conquest over others, can end up transmuting itself into something both wider and more noble, into a feeling of self-confidence, a temporary conquest of human *angst* or an expanded mental perspective which yet remains only half conscious.

Rock-climbing provides innumerable examples of this alchemy. It is the most directly competitive form of mountaineering, yet often takes place in arenas of such breathtaking natural beauty that one can hardly help being reminded of the wider perspective. What begins as the sheer joy of winning may change radically, even into something of spiritual value, without any conscious effort on one's own part.

And in the end this is perhaps the most valuable of all mountaineering's qualities; it presents us with a perspective within which our ego is confirmed without others being belittled. Beating other people can be done in lots of ways but the reward of mountaineering is altogether wider, being a vision of the world which is awesome yet reassuring. For a time there is a saying 'yes' to life rather than 'no', a confidence, a feeling of 'men like Gods'. The value of competition is that it can provide the motive for getting to the frontier, the place where one feels like a God, when otherwise one wouldn't bother. Winthrop Young said that we go to the hills to be reminded of what we have forgotten. True; but there has to be something to persuade us to make the effort. Now, philosophy persuades hardly anyone. Competition, on the other hand, is a great persuader.

To non-participants mountaineering smacks of escapism. To mountaineers it feels more like freedom. One can understand only too well the feelings of the young Kurt Diemberger, school teacher, happy, with no real reason for dissatisfaction. And yet . . . and yet, maddeningly, he is dissatisfied. However good the days he cannot draw himself away from 'the knowledge that no pleasure, no improvisation, can permanently mitigate the monotonous burden of increasing regularity'. He sits in the classroom looking out: 'window periods', like the air-spaces between the window-gratings. There they are, and they are no use to one. What have I done? What should I do? Security . . . a living . . . but time is passing; the sun circles in its course. There is a despairing entry in my diary: 'how much longer can I stand it?'

My young charges have no idea how I feel; we get on splendidly. . . .'

After much agonising Diemberger's answer is the romantic answer – sacrifice security and comfort and strike out heroically. You can do anything, absolutely anything, if you really want to; this is his insight as he leaves the classroom and makes for the Himalaya.

Lord Byron would certainly have approved, and so would Nietzsche, whose call to individual freedom and separation from the herd has resulted in his being more closely associated with mountaineering than any other philosopher. 'Live dangerously!' he says, a sentiment central to the full experience of mountaineering, whatever might be said publicly. For although it is possible to enjoy mountains without risk it can only be done by sacrificing the complete experience of the frontier, the edge between the known and the unknown, and that is the real core. Totally safe mountaineering has its place – for the young an introduction to greater things, for the old a reminder of them – but it is a distortion of the full experience and dishonest to pretend otherwise.

Mountaineering is a pursuit which forces one to think about death, and the only view one *can* take if one is to carry on is that of the romantic hero; that it is precisely by risking life and being prepared to lose it that we prove to ourselves that our lives are worthwhile. 'Man can preserve his dignity only by showing that he is not afraid of anything', wrote the poet and climber Michael Roberts. 'The sacrifice is not necessary; the risk brings no material gain, but it offers something – the exhilaration, the sense of clear vision – which partly excuses the risk.' It is one way to prove that one is capable of going beyond utilitarian values, beyond food, family and material gain, and that beyond them lies something else – not just exhilaration, but a mental and spiritual superiority whose call we can never wholly forget. Many die too late, claimed Nietzsche; 'die at the right time!'

This is not necessarily morbid or disrespectful to life. The mountaineer's real concern is not with death but with freedom in life, in trying to appreciate life more fully and gaining a more solid and immediate sense of existence than occurs under ordinary circumstances. It is simply that to achieve that often means giving up security and courting danger. A love of mountaineering does not imply that one scorns security or that one thinks there is anything particularly praiseworthy about danger. What it does imply is the belief that security has its drawbacks, that security can make us into cowards, and that cowardice is the enemy of self-respect. Only by accepting that, and taking the consequences, can one experience that affirmation of the individual ego that all climbers crave.

It was precisely this call of individuality and ego which led alpine pioneers like Mummery (and he was by no means the first) to dispense with paid guides and begin exploring on their own. It was a significant development in mountaineering history, indicating not that human courage, daring or self-sufficiency were increasing – naturally, courage and self-sufficiency were exactly as they had always been – but that circumstances were changing and had to be allowed for. The earliest pioneers enjoyed an almost completely untrammelled wilderness and, even with guides, had more than enough opportunities in which to feel adventurous, bold and heroic. They were on close, if formal, terms with their guides. They would not have felt, as it is perilously easy to feel on a guided climb today, that they were mere baggage, a nameless person, someone who was simply being dragged to the top as quickly and efficiently as possible. But it is not difficult to see that as unknown terrain was penetrated and as the employer-guide relationship became systematised, mountaineers' egos would suffer. It would become necessary to alter the balance a little if one was to maintain the rewards of the game.

Mummery had no dislike of guides as such. In *My Climbs* he wrote exuberantly of the close shaves he had with his guides Burgener and Venetz, outings which were as much an adventure for them as for their employer. But with increasing numbers this sort of relationship was fast becoming a thing of the past and he didn't like what was replacing it. The guide had been '. . . a friend and adviser: he led the party and entered into all the fun and jollity of the expedition; on the return to the little mountain inn he was still, more or less, one of the party . . .' And now? He had become a 'contractor'. The climb was simply to be 'done', and at the maximum possible speed. Each client would follow exactly the same course, and get exactly the same experiences in return: '. . . the individuality of the Herr is not considered'. Mummery did not climb in order to coo at views but to assert himself. He did not want to play the role of monied luggage, and he had no interest in mere efficiency. His greatest objection to guided climbing was 'the absolute certainty with which the day's proceedings are carried out'. That is a true mountaineer talking, and one who could have come from any age.

Exactly a century after Mummery, ego-affirmation by throwing over the traces was the key to arguably the most brilliant young British mountaineer of the 1980s, Alex MacIntyre. Like Mummery, MacIntyre climbed boldly and uncompromisingly, and he wrote about his adventures in much the same way. In *The Shishapangma Expedition*, which he wrote with Doug Scott just before his death, he emerges as deeply arrogant and egocentric as well as exceptionally determined and talented. But he also manages to convey a great sense of freedom and control over his own life. Perhaps it was an awareness of how little human beings normally achieve in directing their own lives which fuelled his arrogance; he had done rather better. Man is weak when we should be looking at men like Gods, and MacIntyre's epitaph is suitably Nietzschean: 'It is better to live one day as a tiger than a hundred as a sheep'.

Alex's life epitomised the way a sense of freedom can stem directly from ego-achievement. He wanted to climb brilliantly, and when he did so his ego was gloriously affirmed. But the exhilaration which followed depended perhaps too much on physical achievement. I remember him returning in his University days from a lightning visit to Scotland where he had soloed Point Five and Zero gullies on Ben Nevis. A few hours from home I met him in a transport café, his face cracked by a wide and wicked grin. He had a self-imposed time limit of 60 hours for the whole trip and now looked certain to get home in time. One more lift would bring triumph.

None of this is to say that he was necessarily any less aware of the wider perspective than others, or that for someone at the forefront of climbing he was unusually egocentric. What it is to do is to claim that these are the particular aspects of mountaineering which his writing, always talented, often brilliant, conveys most strongly. There is in his writing a

Albert Frederick Mummery (1855–1895) was perhaps the foremost Alpinist of the late nineteenth century, and one of the fathers of modern Alpinism. His preference for small, lightweight ventures of verve and boldness is still entirely relevant a hundred years after his death, and his essays are superbly readable and iconoclastic.
(Photo of Mummery and his daughter courtesy of The Alpine Club.)

'It is better to live one day as a tiger than a hundred as a sheep.' Alex MacIntyre on the south face of Shishapangma in the spring of 1982. MacIntyre was killed a few months later during an attempt on the south face of Annapurna. *(Photo: Roger Baxter-Jones.)*

The entrance to the Kafir village of Bumboret, Nuristan, Afghanistan/Pakistan border
nearly untouched by foreign influences . . . Now, it seems the sculptures have disappea

late 1950s when, in Fosco Maraini's words, 'their world was still quite genuine and
(Photo: Fosco Maraini, 1959.)

disregard of anything peripheral – the land, other people, culture – which in the end seems shockingly narrow, particularly in the context of the breathtaking landscape of Tibet in which his major writing is set. The truth is that climbing is not the only way to expand one's horizons and experience the new; it is not even the only thing about *mountaineering* which offers these rewards. But Alex wrote within a developing *genre* of modernist writing which not only fails to stress mountaineering's gentler illuminations but often deliberately underplays them. And this can be misleading, if not perverse.*

A wider awareness is something we get very readably in Bonington's writings and this makes them attractive in a way MacIntyre's are not, even though as a stylist Bonington is considerably less striking. His writing is 'safe': it says by and large what the public wants to hear and is prepared to buy. But Bonington makes it much clearer that a climber's joy derives not just from climbing but from visual impressions too. The life in a desert land, the newness of it, the huge vistas stretching for miles; these too give a feeling of freedom, and what the climbing does is provide a focus and a nice simple motive. The beauty of the views and the mountain plants hiding among the rocks gain a significance and give a joy precisely because they are experienced in the context of something more serious and in itself less enjoyable. It is climbing which brings the 'clear vision', and without it one would probably remain blind. If it is competition which forces people to climb, it is climbing which forces them to see.

The joy produced by a fine mountain view is not in an heroic mould; there is no personal achievement to celebrate, no sense of having successfully cheated death for another day. Yet it can be just as exhilarating as the brilliant climbing achievement. One of the strengths of mountaineering is that there is a wide choice of 'methods'. If life's intensity could only be captured by grappling with new physical frontiers, mountaineering would soon come to look rather bleak. The only options would be the exploration of new country or the courting of more and more painful or dangerous situations, and whilst the former is becoming increasingly difficult to find, the latter has other disadvantages, to say the least. But the existence of non-heroic forms of excitement and discovery widens the horizon immeasurably. Bourdillon's 'moments' do not only come from exploring physical limits. 'For quite a lot of climbers' says Raymond Greene, 'the most powerful reason [to climb a mountain] is an itch to get to the top of the thing and see what's on the other side.' True – and the reason the summit panorama is exhilarating is that it suddenly makes lots of other quite unrelated things seem possible too. Mountaineers who are both expert and contemplative cannot help being aware of this and it is for them a particularly unsettling experience. Peter Boardman for example explored his physical limits to the full, but that only made him more acutely aware of the mental alternatives.

---

*For powerful and critical comments on Alex's character see, for example, Elaine Brook's writing in her *Land of the Snow Lion* and in Alex's own book.

People who understand the visual alternative to heroism and are at the same time without physical talent are liable to be impatient with climbers. Ruskin is the obvious example. His swipes at The Alpine Club, his comment that mountaineers used the Alps as 'greased poles' over which they clambered mindlessly like children, betrayed scorn and annoyance that anyone should need to be so damned *vulgar*. No-one with an ounce of sensitivity would find any of that necessary.*

For many people, Ruskin included, mountain scenery has a power to suggest expansion and freedom which flat country, even the best, can never match. How does this happen? It may be the distances which mountain prospects command; but then the flats of Holland and Lincolnshire, which Ruskin did not like, also command wide views. Perhaps it is the promise of the unknown: the valley one cannot see into, the peak which remains hidden from view. Perhaps it is the sheer scale of the world which mountains and mountain country alone reveal. Whatever it is, mountain scenery has this exhilarating power quite independently of physical action. It is not egocentric in the sense that competitive success or going where no-one has gone before is egocentric. It does not boost the ego. But it does confirm it. So again the paradox; surrounded by the world's most impressive natural forms one finds that, far from being cowed, one's sense of self actually expands, as Hilaire Belloc expressed so powerfully when he first saw the Alps on his journey to Rome:

> Here were those magnificent creatures of God, I mean the Alps, which now for the first time I saw from the height of the Jura; and because they were fifty or sixty miles away, and because they were a mile or two high, they were become something different from us others, and could strike one motionless with the awe of supernatural things ... To what emotion shall I compare this astonishment? So, in first love one finds that *this* can belong to *me*.

The wish to expand into new worlds underpins mountaineering in all its forms and suggests that it goes much further back than the eighteenth century and western romanticism; it goes back to the dawn of history. What has followed since is a sequence of more or less inevitable events reflecting the urge to explore the new and the possibilities brought about by improved equipment and greater opportunities. When Mummery subtitled the chapter of *My Climbs* which deals with his Grepon ascent 'An inaccessible peak – The most difficult climb in the Alps – An easy day for a lady' he was giving a fair summary of mountaineering history. 'The earliest mountain ascent of which any record has been preserved is the ascent of Mount Ararat by the patriarch Noah'; and Noah, notwithstanding the unusual circumstances of his ascent which are unlikely to be

---

*'The Alps themselves, which your own poets used to love so reverently, you look upon as soaped poles in a beer-garden, which you set yourself to climb, and slide down again with "shrieks of delight".' (*Sesame and Lilies*, 1865.) This is a celebrated remark, though various mountaineering scholars have argued that it overstates Ruskin's case, and that given slightly different circumstances he might well have taken up mountaineering himself.

repeated, thereby started a trend. Hundreds of years before western mountaineers took an interest in the Andes, the Incas had climbed many of the highest peaks; they left unmistakable signs on the high, snow-covered mountains of the Chilean-Argentinian border. One can reasonably speculate whether they might even have climbed Aconcagua, at almost 23,000ft the highest mountain in the world outside the Himalaya. It is possible, for the mountain is straightforward on its northern side. In any event, the urge to expand and discover makes it imperative that mountaineering go forward to new things. Stasis can only mean stagnation.*

At the moment demanding new routes are not in short supply, even on the highest peaks. When the South-West Face of Everest was climbed in 1975 it was, like all such events, hailed as the last great problem. Yet somehow last great problems continue to be found, even on Everest. Lower down the scale many of the 8000m peaks still have important and attractive lines which have not been touched; many of the peaks just under the 8000m level have only been climbed once; many at around the 7000m level have not been climbed at all; and many at 6000m have not even been discovered. And large areas of central Asia and to a lesser extent South America are still imperfectly explored.

New peaks can even be created. Until recently the number of 8000m peaks appeared to be fixed at fourteen, but in an important survey made in 1985 (see *Himalayan Peak Guide, Mountain 104* (1985)), the British mountaineer Alan Rouse was able to define no less than twenty-two. And this is not just a matter of classification; in this context, classification *is* discovery. In the same way the Wetterhorn becomes not one summit but three (in order of height, the Mittelhorn, the Hasli Jungfrau and the Rosenhorn; it is the second, not the first, which rises directly above Grindelwald) or that outstanding Scottish hill An Teallach becomes two (Sgurr Fiona and Bidean a' Ghlas Thuill). That is, secondary summits can be upgraded to separate status. Anyone who enjoys the contemporary sport of 'Munro-bagging' – climbing all the 3000ft mountains in Scotland – knows that the question: When is a subsidiary summit a separate mountain? is not a simple one. And given what powers mountaineering development, it is not a trivial one either. Rouse pointed out that the world's highest mountain horseshoe, formed by Everest, Lhotse and Nuptse contains not two 8000m peaks but four: Lhotse Middle and Lhotse Shar are so difficult of access that they deserve to be regarded as mountains in their own right. Indeed 'Lhotse' means 'South Peak', ie south peak of Everest, and was so named by Mallory; if Lhotse Middle and Lhotse Shar do not deserve separate status, does Lhotse itself?

Another example is Kangchenjunga, the most easterly of the giant peaks. Rising from the forests of the Nepal/Sikkim border, as seen from the old hill station of Tiger Hill

---

*It is this very inevitability which makes interesting mountaineering history very difficult to write. Few events are truly seminal, and even fewer climbs. Expedition books as a *genre* suffer from a similar problem, setting out as they do to relate a series of events – planning; approach; climb; descent; return – which always follow in the same order.

above Darjeeling, Kangchenjunga forms one of the most celebrated of all Himalayan views. But to see it from a distance is to be struck by the fact that it is not a mountain so much as a range of mountains. Indeed, the name Kangchenjunga means 'great treasury of the five snows'. It has at least five summits, and no less than four of these are above 8000m.

Great mountaineers are those who first see these possibilities and who show where the new now lies. Mummery was a great mountaineer; so in our own time is Reinhold Messner, the Tyrolean who has become the first man to climb all fourteen of the world's highest mountains. The idea that Messner might be physically unique could never be convincing, for supermen are no more a reality in mountaineering than in anything else. But there *are* figures whose faith, drive and imagination are extraordinary.*

The reward which great mountaineers take away with them is a particularly strong sense of self, of pure ego. It is encouraged by the belief that 'the masses' experience a relatively poor sense of self because they cling to the herd and refuse to be heroic. But the mountaineer chooses insecurity and the unknown and the result is a clear con-fidence, a feeling of 'men like Gods'. Walking out from the Himalaya after making a brilliant ascent of Gasherbrum I with Peter Habeler in 1975, Messner was confronted by glacier rivers which before the climb would have seemed like major obstacles. But now, buoyed up on the wave of success, obstacles are 'no longer obstacles; they are merely things to overcome'. His self-confidence is supreme now: 'I could go on like this for years, on and on forever'. And Joe Tasker, perhaps the greatest writer on the anguish of climbing on the big hill in modern mountaineering literature, recalls his feelings after his first ascent of the West Face of Changabang with Boardman:

> I packed a few essentials into a rucksack for my journey and raced after the main party who had left an hour before. The day was beautiful, I felt fit and strong, confident and satisfied. I crossed a plateau of grass browning with the arrival of autumn, and delighted in my effortless progress. I wanted the sensation of strength and capability to go on and on . . .

Unfortunately, it never does.

---

*In descending order of height the fourteen 8000ers are: Everest (Sagarmatha, Chomolungma) 8848m; K2 (Mt Godwin-Austen, Chogori) 8611m; Kangchenjunga 8586m; Lhotse 8516m; Makalu 8463m; Cho Oyu 8201m; Dhaulagiri 8167m; Manaslu 8163m; Nanga Parbat 8125m; Annapurna I 8091m; Gasherbrum I (Hidden Peak) 8068m; Broad Peak (Falchan Ri) 8047m; Shisha Pangma (Gosainthan, Xixabangma) 8046m; Gasherbrum II 8035m. 8000m converts to 26,247ft. For comparison, Aconcagua is 22,835ft (6960m), Mont Blanc, the highest mountain in the European Alps, is 15,771ft (4807m), and Ben Nevis, the highest in Britain, 4406ft (1343m).

Arnold Lunn (1888–1974), mountain lover and pre-eminent ski
mountaineer, after a ski ascent of the Eiger. Lunn's love affair with
mountains was wide-ranging, but centred firmly in Switzerland.
(Photo courtesy of The Alpine Club.)

3   The One Crowded Hour of Glorious Life

Why is it that the new is exhilarating in a way which nothing else is? Because the new provides contrast. The professional classes of the nineteenth century found they were refreshed in the Alps, where they could escape for a while the impositions of Victorian respectability; the first rock-climbers were refreshed by the adrenalin surge of struggling with overgrown crags and risking their lives – quite a change from the University libraries and theological discussions which normally occupied them; working men of this century escaped the mills and factories to find a whole new world in the clean air of the Yorkshire and Lancashire moors. And today it seems to be anyone and everyone who finds in the hills escape from 'pressures'.

No-one for whom mountains are an everyday and age-old experience is attracted to them in quite this way. No-one who lives and works in the hills can ever feel quite the same as the city dweller for whom they appear as a sort of promised land. The peasant's subconscious attachment to the land may be stronger than any tourist's, but the peasant can never feel that simple relief of seeing the hills for the first time that comes to modern urban man. And in this sense Wordsworth, who lived for most of his life, including his childhood, in the English Lake District, is not as close to the modern mountain lover as, say, Coleridge, whose natural piety is more strongly coloured by a love of contrast.

The logical development of a love of contrast is a love of extremes. If a little contrast is good, presumably a lot of contrast, and often, is better. So the mountaineer may develop into a dare devil, with a hunger for adrenalin; and where will the process end? Mountaineering is a serious pastime, not because it is physically dangerous but because there are profound insights to be gained from it. It is serious because the appetite for those insights, or for the sheer exhilaration which goes with them, can become overwhelming. Moments of intensity are addictive. Climbing can become a drug.

A moral value has sometimes been claimed for mountaineering in a similar way to war. Like war, mountaineering may help one overcome fear, and with certain provisos this is good. The essential proviso is straightforward: to distinguish between fear and the fear of fear. Freedom from fear is in itself of doubtful value because lack of fear just makes one foolhardy and liable to throw one's life away too cheaply. 'Freedom from the fear of fear, on the other hand, is an ideal which few attain and which all desire', as Arnold Lunn puts it. Why? Because the fear of fear cramps your style. It prevents you seeking the new horizon. It represses rather than liberates.

Moral considerations apart, mountaineering can provide a substitute for the excitement of war and there are several post-war climbers who, writing of the armistice in 1945, record a rather disturbing reaction: however much of a relief, it left a vacuum of excitement which demanded to be filled. The French mountaineer Lionel Terray expressed it candidly in *Conquistadors of the Useless*, and his compatriot Pierre Dalloz summed it up in this way:

> Too much pent-up energy and feeling, now useless, was thrown back at us. We had to find some outlet for it. Climbing came as a revelation to us, just when it was needed, and to it we gave ourselves up, body and soul, while others threw themselves into the pursuit of business, politics or pleasure.

But danger is addictive, and it has the characteristics of any addiction. For one thing, it gives rise to withdrawal symptoms; for another, enough is never enough. It is the problem of Coleridge becoming addicted to opium – a habit which eventually killed him.

Part of the problem is that the extreme life is a form of expansionism, and expansionism never ends. In some forms that hardly matters, indeed it is one of expansionism's great strengths as a philosophy. No-one who loves exploring will ever see everything; there is always another mountain range to explore, another pass to cross. In a thousand years I could not describe the wonders of Himachal, says the sage, and we can rejoice in that. We need not feel it to be a disadvantage, but, on the contrary, the sense of the infinite, which we will never reach, is precisely what attracts. But when our longing takes the form not just of new sensation but of stronger sensation – in a word, when we pursue the extreme life – the fact that it never ends can leave the climber with a serious problem.

In his autobiography *Nanga Parbat Pilgrimage* the Austrian mountaineer Hermann Buhl produced one of the great accounts of the extreme approach to climbing, a catalogue of enormously rewarding but hair-raising escapades from which he only escaped by the skin of his teeth. Buhl's formative years were spent in the Eastern Alps around his home town of Innsbruck, where he demonstrated both a rare talent for climbing and an exceptional ability to endure suffering. These alpine adventures were followed by a *tour de force* which is universally recognised as one of the greatest feats of endurance in mountaineering history: the first ascent of Nanga Parbat, on his own for two days at 8000 metres, without food, water or spare clothing. Perhaps the most remarkable part of Buhl's triumph was not that he climbed the mountain, but that he got back. Having reached the summit in the evening he somehow survived a night out just below the summit before staggering back to safety the next day.

The magnitude of Buhl's feat has never been doubted. Nanga Parbat is the world's tenth highest mountain, and, although the 1953 route up it is technically easy, it is extremely long and Buhl's push to the summit from the expedition's top camp involved a height gain of some 4000 feet and a horizontal distance of three miles, a very long way at that altitude. Performances like that may be equalled, but they are never going to be surpassed. Buhl went to the limit of what is physically possible, and photographs taken when he got back show him as an old man. Indeed it is doubtful if he ever fully recovered from the strain of those two days.

Yet he went on – in 1957 to climb Broad Peak with Diemberger and then to attempt Chogolisa, on which he died. He would never surpass Nanga Parbat, yet there seemed to be no limit to the urge to seek strong sensations. What was enough for one year was not enough for ever. It faded remarkably quickly, even when the experience was that extreme.

Buhl knew all this of course. After Nanga Parbat he had written that even as he was being helped down the mountain by his companions it was already beginning to seem unreal. If only one could hold onto it . . . . But this, it seems, is the difficulty. Each success is not so much an ending as a springboard for something more. Buhl found that the unique satisfaction of hard climbing drove him back again and again, even though 'we knew . . . that climbing purely for its own sake can give no ultimate satisfaction'.

Mummery had gone to extremes on the same mountain more than fifty years before. Buhl was the first man to climb Nanga Parbat; Mummery was the first to attempt it, and in some ways his was as impressive a performance. Buhl's feat, though extraordinary, was not completely without precedent or outside a developing tradition. People had made long and risky climbs to the tops of high mountains before, and, only a year after the Nanga Parbat climb, Buhl's fellow Austrian Herbert Tichy was to triumph brilliantly with a very small team on the even higher peak of Cho Oyu. But Mummery's attempt really was without precedent, and if it was based largely on ignorance of just what he was attempting to do, it still delivered the very special rewards of extreme experience. It was a search for that 'one crowded hour of glorious life', and in that sense was entirely successful. Spirits of Mummery's verve and essential rashness rarely grow old and grey; they die first.

Again, it would seem impossible to surpass the achievement of being the first man ever to reach the summit of the highest point on earth. Yet Sir Edmund Hillary continued to be as enchanted by excitement and adventure after climbing Everest as he had been before. Tall, craggy and impatient for action, Hillary began climbing in his native New Zealand after witnessing the triumphant return of a party from Mount Cook, the country's highest mountain:

> I retreated to a corner of the lounge filled with a sense of futility at the dull, mundane nature of my existence. Those chaps, now, were really getting a bit of excitement out of life. I decided there and then to take up mountaineering. Tomorrow I'd climb something!

That is a shock: to realise how much one is missing. Life sometimes seems to be nothing so much as a colossal con-trick in which one sacrifices the present for some unknown future. And the future never arrives. The backlash is to say we must wake up to life now, now! One must redress the balance: do something, in Longstaff's words, 'to live in every moment of the present'; take on board Shipton's self-justification:

> In these days of upheaval and violent change, when the basic values of today are the vain and

shattered dreams of tomorrow, there is much to be said for a philosophy which aims at living a full life while the opportunity offers . . . nothing can alter the fact if for one moment in eternity we have really lived.

Hillary set about doing that through all sorts of hazardous activities: walking, yachting, crocodile hunting, driving a farm tractor to the South Pole (he was the first man to reach it overland for 46 years), navigating Himalayan rivers, even climbing occasionally. Like John Hunt his fate is to be remembered only for Everest, but like Hunt he has done a great deal else besides. Hillary's life seems to have consisted of an almost desperate series of attempts to keep himself interested, and his books suggest that his reasons for climbing are fundamentally simple: avoid boredom, renew the sense of exhilaration. There is little to suggest spiritual concerns in them, though he admits to a soul-searching and interest in comparative religion that is typical of many people who find themselves dissatisfied with 'normality'. His answer to such dissatisfaction, so far as he reveals it in his writings, is the very direct one of physical exhilaration, with its inevitable partner, dangerous situations entered into and survived. Dougal Haston once remarked that the experienced (and wise) mountaineer is one who has got himself into unwise situations many times and been lucky enough to survive them all, and that's difficult to argue with. Hillary has enough hair-raising near escapes to relate – the drive to the South Pole seems to have been particularly hazardous – but at least they succeeded in staving off the boredom. Back in his Air Force days at the end of the war he had written to his sister that one day he planned to 'write a book and call it *Battle Against Boredom*'. He never wrote the book, but he has lived out the creed.

Extreme climbing is a reflection of a profound element of human nature; that our whole perception of the world, and certainly our appreciation of it, relies heavily on comparing and contrasting. We seem incapable of grasping a situation for what it is, always needing something else to which to relate it. People have been known to volunteer for all kinds of pains and penances because it is so nice when you stop. When Graham Greene escaped death on Berkhamstead Heath his sense of exhilaration was overpowering and life contained an infinite number of possibilities. But not, apparently, for very long. So too, climbers may experience the strongest sensations of relief and thankfulness when they get into extreme situations and pull it off. At that moment, life seems suddenly to be marvellous. But it does not last. It gets forgotten like everything else, so we return to the hills whose lure endures for ever. There is no escape.

Extreme experience makes one realise how blind one is. And it makes one for ever dissatisfied with blindness.

This is far too big a problem to belong just to mountaineering. The writer Colin Wilson has described lucidly how he first became aware of blindness in himself:

One hot day in 1954 I was hitch-hiking up the Great North Road to Peterborough, in a state of fatigue and 'life-devaluation'. . . . I felt so depressed that I did not even feel grateful when a lorry finally stopped for me. After a mile or so, there was a knocking sound from his gearbox, and he explained that he would have to pull in to a garage to have it repaired. So I got out and went on hitching. A second lorry stopped for me. Again, I felt no gratitude or relief. But after about ten minutes or so, an absurd coincidence happened; there was an odd knocking noise from *his* gearbox too . . . And for the first time that day I felt a positive emotion, a feeling of 'Oh *no!*' and a lot of unprintable things. However, he drove on cautiously, and found that the noise stopped when he drove at less than 20 miles an hour. After half an hour of this – both of us listening with trained attention for the noise – he said: 'well, I think we'll make it if we keep going at this speed'. And I suddenly felt an overwhelming sense of relief and delight. And I caught myself feeling it, and noticed its absurdity. Nothing had been 'added to me' in the last half hour, nothing given. All that had happened was that I had been threatened with inconvenience, and the threat had been removed.

What this amounts to is a tendency to take things for granted. We are only really affected by changes in circumstances, not by the circumstances themselves, and it is very difficult for us to appreciate what we have always had. Wilson offers a number of examples of this which all have a flavour of perversity about them yet psychologically ring true, such as the Indian Saint and mystic Ramakrishna who is supposed to have received his first 'vision of God' when about to plunge a sword into himself. Contrast is essential, and perhaps that is why, given a 'flat' existence, we become obsessed with trivialities and will happily grumble about something minor rather than nothing at all.

The twentieth century mystic George Gurdjieff produced an arresting image for the problem when he claimed that the average person spends their whole life in a stupor or 'sleep' and is never really 'awake' at all. If one was awake one would see things for what they really are, or at least realise that most of the time one does *not* see them for what they are. Anyone who is truly awake is acutely aware of their own self and of the extraordinariness of being in the world at all, and is detached from those immediacies of life about which everyone else gets so excited. As it is, most of us live under a form of hypnotism. We are unaware of the true situation, our outlook is subjective rather than objective, our attitudes are determined by personal circumstances and small problems, and most of all we forget death and the irretrievable nature of every moment. Only some sort of shock can get us out of this. Putting the same ideas in a different way: there is a 'threshold of awareness' which must be passed if one is to wake up – and even then, one is liable to do so only temporarily. 'Recent psychology' wrote William James, 'speaks of the threshold of a man's consciousness in general to indicate the amount of noise, pressure, or other outer stimulus which it takes to arouse his attention at all . . .'

Perhaps it was his recognition of this that caused Gurdjieff, in exasperation, to say that 'man will give up anything but his suffering'. For at least suffering makes him feel alive. At least it keeps him awake.

According to Gurdjieff, someone who is truly awake is in a state of consciousness called self-remembering. His follower P. D. Ouspensky explained self-remembering as a sort of simultaneous awareness of oneself and one's surroundings – not one or the other, but both together. It is a state at once detached and yet involved, egocentric yet humble. And the most straightforward way to encourage it is contrast. 'Every kind of emotional moment, emotional shock, makes you realise "I am",' says Ouspensky; '. . . when you are in unusual circumstances it always reminds you of your existence. But in customary conditions we always forget.' It is only in 'unusual circumstances' that the mind is properly awakened and life takes on that visionary quality in which objects almost glow and the world seems full of possibilities. But such states pass and we are soon back in ordinary life, too flat and lacking in strong sensations to sustain anything but a stupor.

The mountaineering experience demonstrates time and again the truth of these ideas. Contrast wakes one up at last, and one looks forward to the pleasures of life with a new strength. On Everest in 1933 Raymond Greene mused on the delights of his favourite London restaurant and a civilised stroll through the Park. Other Everesters have written longingly of the Kharta valley, an oasis of vegetation and colour falling from the east side of the mountain. And I remember a vivid personal experience: spending five days in a snow hole high in the Karakoram whilst a storm raged and we discussed the planning of the perfect meal. Our discussions went on interminably, but they never palled and I was convinced that on our return from the mountain we would put our plans into action. How was it that we had never appreciated the sheer joy of food before? The pleasures to be derived from eating were such that one might well spend the whole of the next summer doing it. One certainly wouldn't be climbing mountains.

Perhaps if it were possible to make the transition instantaneously one would have done all these things. 'I thought as I lay in my tent how delightful it would be if a magic carpet could carry me in seconds from the Rongbuk Glacier to the Hammam in Jermyn Street' wrote Greene. 'My best suit would be awaiting me there. A leisurely Turkish bath, a shave and a haircut, and I would be ready to saunter out into St James's to meet the girl of the moment.' But the reality of the situation is very different. When you are at home you itch to be away; when you are away you want to be home. As Doug Scott has said, you just get used to it. It is a process which can never end, for ambition feeds on success.

The immediate result of extremes is an adrenalin surge, pure excitement. But there is more to it than that, for just as competitive triumph can develop into something wider and more noble, so too can the adrenalin 'high' and the relief that follows it. It can make you see beauty where you were previously blind to it. Wordsworth once attempted to explain how his moments of poetic inspiration arose. The story is told, by De Quincy, that he and Wordsworth were waiting for the Mail Cart from Keswick. Wordsworth put his ear to the ground and listened intently, and when he straightened up his attention was suddenly caught by an early evening star – and immediately, it appeared intensely beautiful. 'Now I can explain to you how I come to write poetry. If ever I am concentrating on something that has nothing to do with poetry, and then I suddenly relax, whatever I see when I relax appears to me to be beautiful.' Something like that happens in climbing. Because it is potentially lethal you concentrate. But when the concentration is released you may see the whole world transfigured with significance. The world glows.

This is the lasting message of *Undiscovered Scotland*, W. H. Murray's classic account of climbing in the 1930s. The combination of being released from the struggle and yet in the sort of impressive situation which mountaineering so often provides opens the visionary faculties very effectively, and the harder the climb the truer this is.

Murray is primarily associated with winter climbing in the Western Highlands, particularly Glencoe, but he did climb elsewhere and in one of his articles he describes a near miss on the Nantillons glacier above Chamonix in the French Alps, a dangerous place which has seen a number of tragedies. Murray and his companion were ascending the glacier in the early morning to attempt the Charmoz when an avalanche very nearly killed both of them. They survived by taking cover in a couple of crevasses.

> We continued our climb, and had an excellent day on the Grands Charmoz. But for a long time after that, if any bearer of ill-tidings had come to me reporting the total loss of everything I possessed in the world I should not have thought the news too serious. I had health and life and the ability to support myself by work. I should not, like the bankrupted financiers of Wall Street or the City, have cast myself from the top window of a skyscraper or more modestly blown out my brains. Life was seen very much in its proper perspective.

That is an outlook of tremendous value, but very difficult to maintain in ordinary life. There is no doubt that one of the reasons we go to the hills is to regain a more 'proper perspective'.

But the question remains: how *much* contrast is necessary? Gratefulness and joy is precisely what one would expect to feel after surviving an avalanche. There is a sense of life being marvellous, of the good things once again remembered. But surely one can feel grateful without going to such extremes? Murray certainly could. Some of his best passages describe climbing on the Isle of Skye, where he seems to have been blessed with almost perpetual good weather and the attendant problems of dehydration. One then returns to the 'wild ecstasy' of chill water. 'I felt that I had never awakened till now to that allegedly familiar quality of water – its wetness.'

And consider Eric Shipton. The moments when Shipton was most himself were not extreme moments on Everest but times of committed but less intense mountain exploration, yet no-one has ever doubted his ability to appreciate life. In fact he seems to have been one of those rare people who never lose their sense of wonder at the natural world. Surely it is Shipton who is to be envied here rather than the high altitude star, the Buhl or the Mummery, who feels driven to seek out extremes again and again, knowing full well that none will satisfy for long. And I am not sure that Buhl or Mummery or their modern counterparts would disagree. Buhl certainly felt that his position required an explanation. Why go on like this? 'Evidently such is my nature.' That almost sounds like an apology. But was it really Buhl's nature which caused him to follow the extreme life? Was it not perhaps the nature of man, which happened to find opportunities through Buhl because of his

W. H. Murray whose memoir of *Mountaineering in Scotland* in the 1930s both defined a style and immortalised its protagonists. *(Photograph of Murray in 1950 by Douglas Scott.)*

abilities? Far from being an expression of free will, extreme climbing is often the complete opposite – a fate out of control, brought about by a perfectly normal human inability to appreciate things combined with an innocent personal talent.

Diemberger, Buhl's companion on Broad Peak and the disastrous attempt on Chogolisa, is the only person to have been on the first ascent of two of the world's 8000m peaks. Like Hillary being first up Everest or Buhl being the first to solo to the summit of an 8000er, that is not only a major feat but also one which can never be repeated by anyone else. Yet still he goes on, to other major ascents, to triumph, finally to a culminating tragedy on K2 in 1986, when an international group of seven climbers found themselves caught on the Abruzzi Spur by a ferocious storm which moved in at the beginning of August.

In attempting K2, the world's second highest mountain and one of the most serious, Diemberger put himself knowingly into a position of extreme vulnerability despite the fact that on Broad Peak some thirty years earlier the hollowness which stalks extreme achievement had already been made clear. On the summit, supposedly the supreme moment and the realisation of all his dreams, he had instead been disappointed and bewildered. 'It was all over. Was I really happy? . . . It had been impressive, the prospect from it overpowering; but the picture in my imagination, my fantasy-summit, outshone it by far.' Diemberger had reached the summit on his own, leaving Buhl slumped in the snow exhausted some distance below, but as he descended he was amazed to see that Buhl had gathered his strength and was slowly approaching. He waited for him, and they returned to the summit together. And this time his feelings were quite different: 'Suddenly everything was so natural that I could laugh about it all; about the fears of all the others down below there, their fears about their lives, my own fear of a little moment ago'. The grasping aspect which normally accompanies major feats had been laid to rest – very rare on an 8000m peak. But then one rarely turns round for a second visit, and it was precisely those unusual circumstances which gave Diemberger the hint of a different way of looking at things. He and Buhl watched the last rays of the sun, as Buhl had done on Nanga Parbat, before descending by moonlight, accepting, without ambition, dread or glory in the mind. A few days later they attempted Chogolisa, where Buhl fell to his death in a blizzard.

On K2 three decades later Diemberger was still searching for 'moments', this time in company with the British mountaineer Julie Tullis. Both reached the summit, then descended to their top camp on the Abruzzi shoulder, still very high on the mountain, in deteriorating weather. And there they were trapped:

> Throughout the night the storm continued '. . . with unrelenting ferocity, and the wind seemed to have some personal malice' against them as though determined to blast them off the mountain. It raged throughout the 3rd and 4th, so fiercely that the stoves would not keep alight, nothing could be cooked or heated, and they were unable to get more than a cupful or two of liquid to drink.
>
> On the morning of the 5th, one of the four tents was destroyed. Houston and Bell crawled with their sleeping-bags for shelter into the other tents, and there were now eight men in three small tents. The same conditions continued throughout the 5th and 6th.

'The one crowded hour of glorious life.' The great Austrian mountaineer Hermann Buhl photographed on the Broad Peak/Chogolisa expedition on which he was killed, four years after his extraordinary solo ascent of Nanga Parbat in 1953.
(Photo: Kurt Diemberger, 1957.)

Still searching for the crystals . . . Now in his early sixties, Kurt Diemberger is one of the most influential of contemporary mountaineers, a pivotal mountain writer, and a great survivor.
(Photograph of Diemberger in the Central Karakoram, July 1979, by John Cleare.)

Kurt Diemberger on Broad Peak during the first ascent, with K2, 'the great crystal', behind. In marked contrast to Everest, K2's reputation has grown since its first ascent in 1954. The Abruzzi ridge, on which the tragedies of 1952 and 1986 were played out, forms the right-hand skyline. The Abruzzi shoulder is the slight easing of angle before the final summit pyramid. *(Photo: Kurt Diemberger, 1957.)*

The words are those of Kenneth Mason, relating the terrible epic of the American expedition which came close to making the first ascent of K2 in 1952; yet the scenario is virtually identical to that of the '86 tragedy in which, after several days of the nightmare, only the two oldest and heaviest climbers, Diemberger and fellow-Austrian Willi Bauer, had the strength to drag themselves to safety.

Since the power extremes have over us is a reflection of the way the human mind is made, everyone is susceptible to the addiction. This is one reason why the voice of responsibility is always so ready to criticise risk. Eminent Presidents of the Alpine Club in its nineteenth century heyday were all the quicker to denounce 'unjustifiable' dangers because they knew they were guilty themselves and they knew the seriousness of the disease. Even the mountaineering aesthetes had dirty hands. Martin Conway, who besides walking and climbing in the Alps made important exploratory expeditions to the Karakoram and elsewhere, was both an artist and an art historian and a man of sensibility, but this did not lessen his vulnerability. In his first Alpine season:

> The air was still; absolute silence reigned; the afternoon sun burnt down upon us with scorching fierceness. A strange agitation invaded all my being. I was no doubt frightened and knew it, and determined that no one else should guess; but there was much more than terror: there was an extraordinary exaltation, such as Ulysses may have felt when he heard the Sirens sing.

But perhaps no-one sums up these dilemmas as well as the late Peter Boardman. Boardman was too much of a thinker to be able to enjoy his climbing without questioning it, and his writings indicate his awareness of the problems more clearly and completely than any other modern writer.

Strong, talented, sophisticated, Boardman was the darling of British mountaineering in the 1970s. As the leading light of Britain's professional mountain guides and National Officer of the British Mountaineering Council, he was one of climbing's key civil servants. And he combined prowess as a mountaineer with an outstanding ability with words. He had been on the Bonington expedition to the South-West Face of Everest in 1975 and reached the summit, the youngest person ever to do so. Altogether, one might have thought, enough to satisfy.

Boardman loved the lifestyle of mountaineering and recognised its deep roots. When he climbed the huge north ridge of Kangchenjunga with only three companions, digging snow-caves was essential in order to escape the hurricane-force winds:

> "You'd never work this hard for anyone else," said Doug.
>   "I always liked den-building as a kid," I said.

And of the West Ridge of Gauri Sankar, which he climbed only a couple of months later, he wrote:

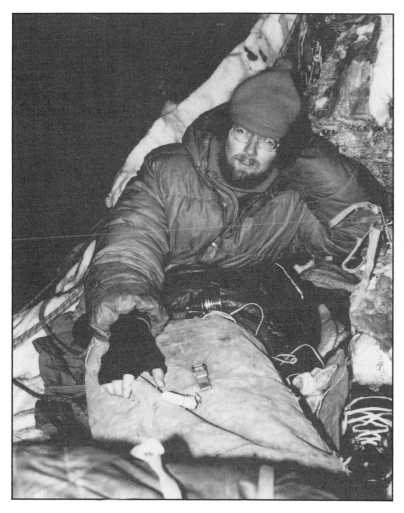

Joe Tasker (1948–1982) during his winter ascent of the north face of the Eiger with Dick Renshaw in 1975. Tasker's early adventures in the European Alps were as intense and rewarding as his later Himalayan achievements; yet the Himalaya ruined the Alps for him and after experience in the greater ranges he could not recapture the Alpine magic.
(Photo: Dick Renshaw.)

Peter Boardman (1950–1982) and his former boss at the British Mountaineering Council, Dennis Gray (foreground), in the 1970s – 'the long hair era'.
(Photo: Dennis Gray collection.)

A child spends hours absorbed in play, building dens and dugouts in trees and mud. The climber constructs his new home high on the mountain, and quickly settles in. Below our perch on the fantastic parapet of the Nid d'Aigle, the sun threw strangely clipped shadows across the southern face, and Guy and I smiled like children.

These primitivist aspects of mountaineering – the bivouac, the day-to-day living, the effort to do it all as efficiently and with as little waste of energy as possible – these answered a deep need in Boardman which could not find satisfaction in the normal adult world. But there is more to mountaineering than den-building, and Boardman's ability made it almost inevitable that he should pursue a course leading him into more and more extreme situations. In doing so he tasted all the rewards; and it is part of his achievement to have conveyed in words his total awareness of both their transient and their compulsive character. The pure sensation of sheer joy and boosted ego comes after any big climb and is an infinitely precious moment. After Kangchenjunga.

> We lay down on the grass amid yellow flowers ... After many weeks in a barren world of snow and rock, we were in a garden, beautiful and haunting as though pre-visited. We slept deeply until mid-afternoon, and woke refreshed. That sleep was Kangchenjunga's parting gift.

No-one expresses it better. The cruel forces with which one rashly decided to tangle have miraculously relented for a little longer and for a short while time almost stands still, the joy of it is so intense. But Boardman is too wise to expect it to last and is in continuous doubt whether those few exceptional moments are really worth the candle. In any case, he has a social conscience; and what does climbing *contribute?* He scorns the way people admire his courage. What is courage? Certainly not doing what you want to do and are good at. High altitude mountaineering may look heroic, but the real heroes are the millions of people who take on the responsibility of raising a family, who struggle with the boring problems of life in the middle lane, *who accept ordinariness*.

Walking out from Kangchenjunga, the expedition stands aside as hundreds of Nepalese come down the trail with an air of purpose and celebration:

> They were going to a wedding and stared back at us blankly. Hindus do not understand foreign tourists. No doubt, to them we were just paisa-wallahs, who had so much money they could travel – not to visit relatives or to attend a wedding, but just to see new things, without knowing anything and leaving their world and family to wander like cows.

Suffering such self-disparagement despite having completed a brilliant climb, he comes to the only possible conclusion: that it is only through such contrasts that one can ever appreciate 'ordinary' life properly. *In extremis* with Joe Tasker on Changabang he had spoken of 'playing to the audience of my mind', surely one of the best phrases ever found for Gurdjieff's self-remembering. Later, when they returned to Base Camp triumphant, they experienced the contrast of another expedition which had been rather less fortunate: four Americans climbing a nearby peak had been killed. And the bleak truth was that 'the deaths of the four climbers had made us feel alive with every breath. This was the sensation of life – the sense that we remained'. Extreme climbing had taken them back to another mentality, harsh, but at least vital and alive. To be closely involved with death is to return with a vengeance to a concentration on the things that really matter.

There is no question of Boardman's being a nihilist; the accusation of a death-wish would be an affront. He knows the value of extreme climbing, but he also knows that its only real value is as a means to an end: to re-awaken a sense of wonder. After the Kangchenjunga expedition he has three months before the next Himalayan assignment, and appreciates it 'with the intensity of a soldier home on leave'. The short term is marvellous; it is the long term implications which prey on his mind. Each individual climb is satisfying like nothing else in life, but when you stand back from the exhilaration of the moment and look at it all as a whole, year after year, the picture is worrying. Before he leaves for Kangchenjunga someone tells him he is becoming over-reliant on extremes, and like any jibe that hits the target it sticks in his mind. 'Wordsworth loved mountains, but wandered most of his life beneath the fifteen-hundred-foot contour. He had not needed experience of such violent stimulants, such risk, to shock him into moods of awareness.' So why do I?

But however you get out of extreme experience, you do not do it by rational argument. Boardman was in that position which Shipton had managed to avoid. He was talented, loved big mountains, and had the opportunity; how could he avoid going on? Realising the dangers is never enough. One may believe that a life of endless extremes is not the true end of life, but the power of extremes is way beyond arguments. It touches us on a deeper level. One sees this again and again in mountain writings.

'Back again, eh Alan?' says Greg Child, meeting Alan Rouse in Pakistan when both are *en route* to big objectives.

'Yes, back again. Why do we do it?'

'God, I can't work it out.'

To work it out one must accept that pleasure and happiness are not the same thing, and that there is a tradition of human thought – asceticism – which recognises that. The ascetic is not the same as the puritan. The puritan thinks the pursuit of pleasure bad, whereas the ascetic simply regards it as not the most effective way to attain happiness. Ascetics believe that happiness is inextricably linked with pain, as one might expect if grasping life properly relies on contrast.

The philosophy of asceticism has an important place in mountaineering. As Arnold Lunn has pointed out, the word originally meant exercise. 'To the Greek the athlete was the typical ascetic, for he exercised his body by sacrificing the pleasure of self-indulgence to the happiness of self-discipline.' Why trudge over wet cold hills in the rain when you could be sitting in front of a warm fire? One might say: because you have recognised the value of pain. It is written on the face of any Sunday fell-walker after a hard but satisfying day. Walkers are not puritans, but they know that temporarily shunning comfort gives access to a new happiness. And that also applies to climbers. 'Why do we do it?' asks Rouse, and the answer is the same: to gain a new perspective on life and thus a happiness which hedonism cannot give. Rouse was as much of a pleasure seeker as anyone, but he was also a part-time ascetic. That is a typical mountaineer's solution.

Asceticism certainly has psychological and physiological effects. Everest climbers are ascetics, and in 1933 Frank Smythe was to experience something which has since been recorded many times at high altitude:

> All the time that I was climbing alone I had a strong feeling that I was accompanied by a second person. This feeling was so strong that it completely eliminated all loneliness I might otherwise have felt. It even seemed that I was tied to my 'companion' by a rope, and that if I slipped 'he' would hold me. I remember constantly glancing back over my shoulder, and once, when after reaching my highest point, I stopped to try and eat some mint cake, I carefully divided it and turned round with one half in my hand. It was almost a shock to find no one to whom to give it. It seemed to me that this 'presence' was a strong, helpful and friendly one ...

On Everest forty-two years later Doug Scott had a similar experience, and so did Buhl on Nanga Parbat. Whether such experiences are due simply to lack of oxygen is not known, but they would seem to be the result of privation of one sort or another. At high altitudes there is the privation not only of oxygen but of food, water and sensory stimulus. The sights and sounds and smells of the natural world, of birdsong and running water, trees and flowers, are completely absent. Perhaps that frees the brain for other things. And when one returns to lower levels one then knows a new intoxication – the intensity of life that follows when a self-imposed asceticism is relaxed.

Joe Tasker, Boardman's partner on Changabang, K2, Kangchenjunga and finally Everest, knew all about the intoxication of asceticism. He was brought up in a Catholic seminary and took up climbing in his teens. He found that climbing was not only pleasurable but that its dangers and difficulties exerted a strange fascination which grew rather than diminished as his achievements increased. The idea of physical penance is deep in Tasker's writings, so deep that one inevitably looks for its source in his upbringing. And it gave to his climbing both an extreme and a compulsive character.

Is this the freedom mountaineers are looking for? As he leaves the valley to begin his first climb on the international stage, a winter ascent of the North Face of the Eiger, Tasker looks enviously at the skiers, happy hedonists all, and wishes he did not have to go through something so much less pleasurable in order to feel satisfied. It is a story which is to be repeated time and time again on his subsequent climbs in the Himalaya.

The first of these is his ascent with Dick Renshaw of a difficult new route on Dunagiri (23,185ft) in the Indian Himalaya in 1975. The Dunagiri climb contrasts strongly with the British expedition to the South-West Face of Everest the same year. Everest '75 was a very large affair, a triumph of organisation, and above all a logical culmination. The ascent of the South-West Face itself was a fine piece of climbing which extended technical difficulties to new altitudes. But the expedition's approach was not new. Indeed, it had much in common with the first ascent of Everest in 1953.

Tasker's and Renshaw's adventure was rather different, and began with the overland drive from Manchester in an old Ford van. The pair were beset by financial stringencies and a shortage of time, and set off up the mountain without waiting to acclimatise properly. They were climbing almost as they would in the Alps, and, as with Mummery on Nanga Parbat eighty years earlier, it was the Alpine comparison which almost proved their downfall. They set out with six days' food and finally reached the summit on day six suffering badly from exhaustion. The descent became a long drawn-out nightmare and Renshaw contracted frostbite in his fingers. Alone, and on their first venture to the Himalaya, they were out of control and fighting for their lives. On the walk-in to the mountain Tasker had felt he would give almost anything to climb it, but now he vowed 'never again to get far away from the basic essentials of life. Comfort was what I promised myself forever, total self-indulgence, never far from warmth and liquid and food. A life of ease, a life of luxury, was what I wanted and I would never put it at risk again'. Descending the final glacier in a state of delirium he sees ahead the enormous West Face of Changabang, harder than anything ever attempted in the Himalayas. But it holds no interest. Far from wanting to climb it, he is convinced he will never want to climb again.

How mistaken! That image of Changabang has entered his mind, and the certainties which were formed in days of pain are to dissolve frighteningly quickly. He recruits Peter Boardman for a two-man attempt and within a year is back in India, where nothing has changed, least of all his own dilemmas. On the climb itself, a landmark in Himalayan mountaineering, 'Over and over again I asked myself what I was doing there, and made another promise that this would be the last time'. Even on the rare rest days at Base Camp the worry of it all, and above all the knowledge that it was self-imposed, 'imbued me with a depression which made me blame Pete for everything that went wrong'.

Tasker's case demonstrates both the intoxication of asceticism and the dilemma posed by being good at something which has no end. 'For nearly two years I had been totally absorbed with climbing three mountains', he was to write. 'Each one had represented something different, each one had been at that moment, in its own way, the greatest test I could conceive of. Each test had been passed and I was left bewildered. I was alarmed to have succeeded; in a way it would have been more reassuring to have failed. Instead success left me with an uneasy, unsettling question about where to go next; ... Where would it all lead? What had I gained from the last two years if all that was left to me was an indefinable dissatisfaction?'

Tasker understood the problem perfectly. It was not the appetite for new sensation, but the appetite for *stronger* sensation. It was not that there was no end in sight but that his climbing took him into more and more extreme and dangerous situations each of which became merely a prelude to the next.

Here is the difference between someone whose first love is mountain country – Shipton, say – and the extreme climber. A piece of new country is satisfying in itself, and it is a perverse person who, visiting somewhere new, finds himself thinking 'Yes, but this is not as fine as . . .' Such perversity invades the mind certainly, but it can be recognised as just that: an invasion. It is not an attitude which is essential to an appreciation of wild country, and though such places are doubtless attractive to us partly because they stand in contrast to our normal environment, this is not the whole of it. Wild mountain country has qualities within itself which are valuable to us.

But it seems this is less so for the kind of extreme situation into which Tasker explored. The extreme situation has, as it were, no content of its own; its power is derived from its sheer otherness, with all the attendant disadvantages. It is nothing less than one of the key tragedies of human nature. 'The man who has double my salary is doubtless tortured by the thought that someone else in turn has twice as much as he has, and so it goes on', wrote Bertrand Russell. 'If you desire glory, you may envy Napoleon. But Napoleon envied Caesar, Caesar envied Alexander, and Alexander, I daresay, envied Hercules, who never existed.'

After Changabang, Tasker went on to climb Kangchenjunga and attempt K2 before disappearing, with Boardman, on the North-East Ridge of Everest.

The K2 climb, in which Tasker, Boardman and Renshaw were avalanched and pinned down by storms close to the summit, was as nightmarish and near the edge as Dunagiri. Afterwards, Tasker experienced the same expansion of consciousness he had felt after previous climbs. Then he starts reading *Shogun*, a blockbuster novel of adventure and romance in medieval Japan. He becomes obsessed with it, fascinated by its depiction of violence, the cheapness of life, the simplicity of man behaving as an animal. Walking away from the mountain and towards home,

> I shared the feelings of the Samurai brought back honourably from his suicide and knew the exalted state he would have been in on his reprieve. . . . I felt wealthy, blessed with fortune beyond measure. The body I walked in was weak but it did not matter, the pain of movement was only another proof that I was alive, a sign of new life.

But one forgets. It is like the man who thinks it will be marvellous to be a millionaire, becomes one, and then cannot recall his previous life. Without something to compare with, how can you enjoy it? Even the shocks of pain and danger administered on K2 did not produce permanent change.

'To experience adventure is to heighten perception', the British climber Pat Littlejohn has written, and that means adventure with a degree of danger in it. This is the truth expressed by Ouspensky when he says that it is only in moments of danger or other shocks that man wakes up out of his sleep. Then he is alive, in the sense that a visionary like William Blake is always alive, and everything he sees is vivid and significant. It is part of the mountaineering solution to use danger for this purpose and, without an acceptance of that, mountaineering is not mountaineering; it is simply exercise, or a pleasant view. That is why mountaineers can be accused of blindness; only danger takes them towards certain frontiers, into 'the Undiscovered Country'.*

But the question once again: how much danger, how much contrast? Perhaps there is a point beyond which the promise of greater reward is an empty promise. After Alan Rouse soloed *The Boldest* in North Wales in 1970, one of the most difficult rock climbs of its time, he felt so exhilarated, so drugged by adrenalin, that his legs were weak and rather than try to walk down he descended on his backside. After Chris Preston made the first ascent of *Suicide Wall* in the 1940s, the boldest and most difficult climb of its time, he was so elated that he crashed his motorbike on the way to the celebrations. But lots of weekend climbers have had strong experiences without taking such risks. Being an outstanding climber can be an unenviable fate, for if you have the talent to do these things you will feel compelled to try. They are intimations of the infinite, and such things are dangerous. And it is the outstanding climber for whom they are most dangerous. Tasker was trapped in a *cul-de-sac* because his very sense of self became tied to outstanding climbing achievement. After the K2 expedition, 'rather than being deterred by the ordeal, I realised more clearly than ever before that climbing mountains was what I wanted to do. The reasons are not easy to define; the closest I can come to explaining them is that it makes me the person I am; going to the absolute limit of one's capabilities in anything is always satisfying.'†

If the struggle to reach the infinite is almost unavoidable for outstanding climbers, for the less talented it is still a temptation.

> Who has known heights and depths shall not again
> Know peace – not as the calm heart knows
> Low, ivied walls, a garden close,
> The old enchantment of a rose.

One becomes enchanted instead, and much more perilously, by mountains. One

---

*In *Hamlet* (Act III, Scene i) 'the undiscovered country' is the world beyond death. Arnold Lunn used the phrase (*Mountain Jubilee*, chapter 5) as the title of an essay describing a near-fatal accident: 'There is a country from which no traveller returns, but it may be that a fleeting glimpse of what lies beyond is revealed to those who have approached most closely to the frontier.' My own use in this book is wider. The undiscovered country is not necessarily beyond death; it is simply beyond our normal everyday selves.

†These sentiments echo those of one of the great public heroes of mountaineering, George Mallory. Following his 'Because it is there' comment, Mallory was to write: 'I suppose we go to Mount Everest, granted the opportunity, because – in a word – we can't help it. Or, to state the matter rather differently, because we are mountaineers. Our case is not unlike that of one who has, for instance, a gift for music. There may be inconvenience, and even damage, to be sustained in devoting time to music; but the greatest danger is in not devoting enough, for music is this man's adventure.' (Quoted by Robertson in *George Mallory*, chapter 9).

thinks for example of Julie Tullis, who spent several years of her life trying to climb K2, succeeded, and died on the descent. Herbert Tichy spent most of his life as a mountain wanderer and took no interest in high peaks until he attempted Cho Oyu in 1954. Yet once he got close, the magnetism was extraordinary. He had loved the foothills, the grey-brown vistas of rolling Tibetan hills,

> . . . but now that I gazed into the vastness of the sky above Tibet, I suddenly felt different. I wished to press forward into that sky recklessly and even though it would suffer us only on its circumference . . . I wanted now to get as close to it as my limited powers allowed. There before my eyes was Cho Oyu, and its ridges were ladders into that longed for sky. Suddenly I had become a fanatic to climb them.

And of course there is Noel Odell's experience on Everest. Odell climbed in support of Mallory and Irvine when they made their attempt on the summit in 1924, and the days he spent high on the mountain, first climbing up a day behind the assault party and then returning to the highest camp alone to look for them, have passed into mountaineering folklore. Odell believed he saw Mallory climbing on the crest of the North-East Ridge of Everest on the day of the summit attempt, though there can be no certainty. As all climbers know, it is very easy to mistake rocks for climbers and to be convinced there is movement when there is none. He descended to the glacier but returned to the highest camp two days later. He was extremely well acclimatised by this time and found the expedition's oxygen apparatus of no benefit. After spending the night alone at 27000 feet he continued some distance up the mountain but, finding no sign of Mallory or Irvine or what had become of them, signalled his failure to Base Camp and prepared to descend. But not before he had experienced something even more perilous than the cold and wind of Camp 6:

> . . . I glanced up at the mighty summit above me . . . It seemed to look down with cold indifference on me, mere puny man, and howl derision in wind-gusts at my petition to yield up its secret – this mystery of my friends . . . If it were indeed the sacred ground of Chomolungma – Goddess Mother of the Mountain Snows, had we violated it – was I now violating it? . . . And yet as I gazed again another mood appeared to creep over her haunting features. There seemed to be something alluring in that towering presence. I was almost fascinated. I realized that no mere mountaineer alone could but be fascinated, that he who approaches close must ever be led on, and oblivious of all obstacles seek to reach that most sacred and highest place of all. It seemed that my friends must have been enchanted also . . .

But the summit, even the summit of the world, has a habit of playing false. After the Americans Willi Unsoeld and Thomas Hornbein made the first traverse of Everest in 1963 Hornbein wrote of 'the suspicion that maybe there was something more, something beyond the three-dimensional form of the moment. If only it could be perceived'. But it seems it never can be; not in this way. As one approaches, the 'something' merely retreats further, and even on Everest things remain maddeningly mysterious and incomplete. Diemberger found just the same on Broad Peak, as did Boardman on Kangchenjunga;

'I should be thinking great things,' I thought.
But none came.

Lower altitudes can be just as dangerous. In his poem *The Cragsman* Winthrop Young
writes:

> In this short span
> between my finger-tips on the smooth edge
> and these tense feet cramped to the crystal ledge
> I hold the life of man.
> Consciously I embrace
> arched from the mountain rock on which I stand
> To the firm limit of my lifted hand
> the front line of time and space:–
> For what is there in all the world for me
> but what I know and see?
> And what remains of all I see and know
> if I let go?

These lines express a startling feature of rock-climbing: incredibly, at moments when
one knows the consequences would be serious, many of us have felt a very strong urge to
jump off. Even solo climbers have reported feeling it. It has nothing to do with brashness
or over-confidence, and it is not a question of being unaware of the consequences. In my
experience it is frightening precisely because it is created against all one's reason, and yet
one never quite trusts oneself not to act on it. It may be that the psychological effect of a
spectacular rock climb is to buoy one up on the heady feeling of having issued a challenge
to life itself; feeling like a God, one makes the dangerous mistake of believing one *is* a God.
Most rock-climbing is safe enough, but it creates a very good illusion of being dangerous.
The climber seems to be triumphing over his own mortality, and perhaps the urge to jump
off is just the natural extension of that: the wish to extend the thing further, to extrapolate,
to expand. One is curious. What *will* happen next?

Every climber has had days when the pleasures of a good climb were perversely spoilt by
thoughts of what might have been. The better things go the more you raise your sights.
One March day I went to the winter corries of the Cairngorms to climb ice. Coire an
Lochan was empty but for the two of us, and my heart sank to see the sheer corner of
Savage Slit in perfect condition. But I was frightened of falling from those walls and
breaking my back on one of the great chockstones which block the corner, so I turned
away. We went to another climb, still hard, and struggled to the top in a rising storm.

It is madness to set off on a climb of which you are positively frightened, yet at the end of
the day I couldn't let the image of that corner go. I could have done it; I could have bridged
up those ice-encrusted walls . . . I had never considered the route before, but now it
suddenly seemed important. It plagued my memory for weeks, taking the pleasure from
the day.

Above: Edmund Hillary, not surprisingly looking thin, with Eric and Diane Shipton on the terrace of Eskdale O.B. Centre in the Lake District, June 1953. Shipton (1907–1977), arch-romantic and lover of small, informal expeditions, was ousted from the leadership of the '53 Everest expedition when it became clear that Britain might not get another chance and that what mattered now was not mountaineering ethics, but *getting to the top.* When the successful expedition returned to England one of its first ports of call was to Shipton, who was Warden of Eskdale. *(Photo: John Lagoe.)*

Right: Eric Shipton, with that eternal question mark so apparent between his eyebrows, and his trusted Sherpa, Angtarkay, also looking reflective, in India in the 1970s. *(Photo courtesy of Mrs Phyllis Wint.)*

4 Return to the Primitive

Mountaineering prompts an ineradicable streak of nostalgia, a dislike of progress and change which runs deep and affects the front-runner as well as the average performer. So what do they fear, these people who prefer the past and see in contemporary climbing the destruction of everything worthwhile?

Fears for the future have existed since mountaineering began, but that does not mean they should not be taken seriously. The reactionary trait is a fundamental one, and it means something. Sometimes it is mere jealousy, envy of the successful or blindness and stagnation of the individual; but beyond these lies the realisation that mountaineering is not only about new horizons, least of all new horizons of extreme peril, but includes another element, related to a sense of 'belonging' in the world, which can easily be swamped by egocentricity, and the loss of which would ruin everything. And mountaineers believe they have discovered something about this 'oneness', or sense of identification, which is worth stating explicitly: you cannot feel it in the civilised world, only in the primitive. The town will not do, only the country.

Eric Shipton was well aware that it was really this rather than climbing which attracted him to the unspoilt places of the world. 'There is nothing unusual in the feeling for wild country which has been the chief and most constant influence shaping the course of my life', he wrote. 'Those dreams in early childhood of chasing the moon over the wooded spurs of the Nilgiri Hills were symptomatic; the emotions they engendered have been repeated again and again through the years in a sense of fusion with the surrounding wilderness . . .'

Shipton was primarily a mountain traveller and explorer rather than a technical climber, yet he never seems to have felt sad about this, or jealous of the technical achievements of some of his friends. On the contrary, he was shrewd enough to realise that hard climbing misses something. Everest in particular came to represent an undesirable narrowness of outlook. He far preferred wandering around the lower slopes, peering into odd corners of unexplored glaciers, feeling free; climbing peaks, as high and as hard as you can, has a way of elbowing all that out. So pity the man who is so talented he never escapes from it!

Shipton's 'sense of fusion' is nothing less than the mystic vision, and is the deepest reward of the mountain-walker. In practical terms the question which follows is of course this: how wild does it have to be? Shipton devoted his life to exploring lands which were true wildernesses by anyone's reckoning: Africa, Patagonia, the Himalayas. But Sunday fell-walking in the Lake District can provide a feeling of fusion too, and though this is country rather than town it certainly isn't wilderness. In fact much of what is most central to the Lake District's charm – old stone buildings and walls, roads which weave round the lie of the land rather than through it, copses and fields which lap the valley sides – all of this we have made.

The essential element, the common factor which connects the Himalayas with the Lake District, is a sense of nature's mastery. In the Lake District human activity is very evident but that does not prevent our delight, because we still feel that it is the rhythms of the natural world which are in control rather than ourselves. The stone-enclosed fields are delightful precisely because they show humanity coming to terms with the hills rather than being crudely used for our short-term fancy. Quarrying on the other hand can seem like rape, for here it is made clear that the hills no longer rule and the comfort of the Great Outdoors that we seek, the feeling that nature decides and we accept, has been thrown out. To be comforting the natural world does not have to be static but it does have to change in its own time and not in ours. In a recent book about rock-climbing David Craig had pointed out that one can delight in change, but only if it is evolutionary rather than revolutionary:

> ... since 1983 a ten-foot pendant fang has dropped off a fine steep route called Sostenuto and made its start much harder. But frost and spate and drought are to be expected. When you climb in such a place, you are working with the grain of nature, immersed in its atmosphere, and your very heartbeat feels eased into more inevitable, less forced rhythms.

A fang of rock dropping off a climb is a sign that nature has its own time scale, its own moment for doing things, and we feel, at least in our contemplative moments, that to accept these, to rejoice in them even, is wisdom. Changes that we make ourselves are very different. They remind us that the human race can step outside evolutionary time and impose itself. This is not welcome to either Shipton (the explorer) or to Craig (the rock-climber), and the gloomy predictions of the nostalgic and reactionary begin to look justified.

When we go to the hills we do not attain joy by imposing ourselves, because that implies responsibility. On the contrary, we want to forget our responsibilities for a while and submerge ourselves in something greater:

> ... when I sit on a six-inch ledge with my feet dangling above a two hundred-foot drop, the hart's-tongue fern and dwarf hawthorn a few inches from my eyes, the air smelling of moss, wood-pigeons clattering out of the tree-tops down below, then at least for a time I have grafted myself back into nature, and the sense of rightness achieved, or regained, is unmistakable.

The mountaineer's sensibility to nature has its deepest roots in timeless traditions of nature mysticism, but in terms of cultural fashion it springs from eighteenth century romanticism. Romanticism was a broad reaction against the unqualified belief in the powers of rational mind and reason which seemed to be increasingly gripping civilised man. So: if civilisation was bad, what was good? Primitivism, obviously, particularly a primitivism which included those characteristics such as spontaneity, naturalness and faith in the emotions which seemed to be increasingly lacking in contemporary civilisation.

Primitivism may be all in the mind or one can attempt to live it, and the eighteenth century saw merit in both. But it is back-to-nature as something to *do* – the primitive lifestyle as opposed to trying to think oneself into the primitive mentality – which is the mast to which mountaineering stakes its colours. The mountaineer is someone who believes that the benefits of spontaneity, naturalness or whatever else might accrue from primitivism are to be got by going there rather than by imagining it.

This attitude is a part of the uneasy relationship between active mountaineering and imagination which Boardman, and before him, Ruskin, was so well aware of. It is certainly enough to set mountaineering apart from 'high' Romanticism, that is, Romanticism as a purely aesthetic or artistic movement. For the high Romantic the crux of the thing is not a geographical place like a Pacific paradise or a rural idyll, but a mode of thinking and feeling brought about by imagination. This is the sphere of meditation in all its myriad forms. It uses the imagination purely; man becomes sufficient unto himself. But the mountaineer's creed is crucially different. It aims to encourage new modes of thought and feeling, but only by using outside stimulus. We return to the hills to be reminded of what we have forgotten; also to feel again those things which we find too subtle to be remembered and which *have* to be experienced.

It is easy to exaggerate the primitivist urge. Our ancestors spent most of their energies trying to escape its realities, and we would be doing the same if we did not lead a generally civilised and comfortable existence. But to say that civilisation has actually created the attraction would be going too far, and one of the things that justifies this belief is our modern realisation that primitivism involves not only the experiencing of a more primitive life-style but also of more primitive ways of thought for which some of our most important thinkers would claim a permanent and fundamental importance. Carl Jung for example believed that '. . . every civilised human being, however high his conscious development, is still an archaic man at the deeper levels of his psyche'. He believed that the archaic man within each of us still demands expression, unchanged by culture or education.

Not that everyone agrees with him. Freud regarded many of Jung's archaic needs as neuroses, malformations of the individual with no essential basis at all. And clearly there are many people in the world today who feel no need whatsoever to return to the primitive. By no means everyone longs to escape to the wilderness and commune with nature for the good of their soul. All one can say for certain is that many, very many, people do, and that their longing seems to be more serious and more deeply felt than any mere 'escape'.

One of the attractions of a return to the primitive is a sense of simplification and thus of freedom – freedom from the endless complications and decisions of modern life. It is not just that primitive people do the one thing, the only thing, but that they think the one thing, the only thing. According to Jung such people do not consciously think; the thoughts come to them intuitively, and this because their whole mental life is rooted in the way things are. Life presents them with a *fait accompli*; they must live and work within the situation as it is, and there is no time for western *angst*, for wishing that things were different. They are what they are and they are immediate. Primitive people must do this and they must do that, or they will starve. The environment is that real.

But if this is a cruel reality it is also a mentally simplified one. Moral anguish becomes irrelevant, and the primitive mentality is thus essentially amoral. The universe is not good and it is not bad, and wondering about such things is little more than a diversion for those who have lost contact with the primary facts of life. The universe just *is*. What is important is that we should simply submit, such a submission implying that 'the world' is more powerful than we can ever hope to be. We can worship it by all means, and we can perform rituals, but we do so as supplicants; we can remind ourselves of our dependency, but we cannot change it. That, indeed, is one of the prime sources of our religious feeling.

The crucial point is to get back into contact with the things that really matter. There are only a handful of them, yet oddly enough they are what we seem to lose sight of most easily. Simply surviving is the root, and, after that, trying to eliminate pain and danger. These are not matters we normally give much attention to, but returning to them refreshes one's appetite for life enormously. Most serious mountaineering takes place against a background of danger and discomfort, but only so as to provide something against which one can then play the game of trying to get as comfortable and as safe as possible. There has to be something to kick against. Life in the mountains gives you the opportunity to make use of all sorts of subtle tricks for looking after yourself. Boardman called it 'serious play'; this is what he was doing building a snow-hole with Scott on Kangchenjunga, digging out a platform for the tent on Gauri Sankar. Serious play is a good phrase, because in bringing out the apparent contradictions of return to the primitive it also brings out its depth. In 'normal' life, perhaps because we are so tied up in our own little world, we are convinced we can 'do'; if only we could decide *what* to do. Life demands that we make decisions and we are convinced these decisions matter. Yet simultaneously we are forced to despair, because nothing makes any difference; cause and effect are too tenuously connected. We cannot change anything. The world is too complex, and everyone is pulling in opposite directions.

Mountaineering can be an antidote to all that because the game is being played against real problems for once, not against the man-made, utterly trivial problems which seem to constitute so much of life. You may die if you decide wrongly. Yet at the same time it is a seriousness which is free, even carefree. When one makes decisions in the mountains they are important enough to make one feel truly alive yet they don't produce the sort of anguish which inevitably accompanies a belief in one's own omnipotence. In mountains it is always worth trying to mould events, to exert will, yet in the end something greater hangs over everything. The result is that beyond a certain point one surrenders responsibility for events and becomes fatalistic. 'What more can I do?' takes over. One has self-determination, yet under the widening perspective which the world's wild places encourage, fate has the last word and nothing matters.

When the French climbed Annapurna I in 1950 – the first success on an 8000m peak – two of the summit team, Maurice Herzog and Louis Lachenal, contracted terrible frostbite. On the summit the exhilaration and the beauty swept all else away:

> Our hearts overflowed with an unspeakable happiness.
> If only the others could know . . .
> If only everyone could know!

On the descent Herzog is 'still blissfully floating on a sea of joy'. But later, when the extent of his frostbite has become apparent and he thinks he is going to die, elation has been replaced by a vast resignation:

> There is a supernatural power in those close to death. Strange intuitions identify one with the whole world. . . . All would end well. I should remain there, for ever, beneath a few stones and a cross.

Our ancestors faced fundamental problems such as how to survive and how to get enough to eat which we rarely experience today and which, for all their drawbacks, offered a kind of simplicity we still crave. In mountaineering we create such a simplified reality artificially, by making a distinction between tactics and strategy. We commit ourselves to a strategy – to climb this mountain, to cross that piece of country – and having done so we are left with the freedom to choose our tactics. Strategic decisions may have moral complications, but tactics are nothing to do with morality; they are to do with practicality. So by defining the strategy and only allowing ourselves to think about tactics we simplify the mental life and avoid the questions with no answers.

Chris Bonington has expressed this well: the satisfaction, relief even, of a simple primitive aim which leaves the dilemmas and the questioning far behind. Nowhere in his writing has Bonington seriously attempted the strategic question, Why climb at all? and he is probably wise in this; he is no philosopher. But he is good on the freedom of tactics. Involved in a first winter ascent on the North Face of the Eiger, he and Mick Burke landed on the summit by helicopter in order to meet the climbing team who were approaching the top in the teeth of a storm. Whisked from the comfort and security of their hotel to the savagery of the mountain, they dug a snowhole in darkness:

> Eventually I found a snow bank, brought Mick across to me, grabbed the shovel and started digging. At least I was able to keep warm as I worked away in the shelter of the snow, while all Mick could do was to sit, huddled outside, waiting for me to dig out enough snow for him to creep in behind me. There was an odd sort of enjoyment about the entire venture. Perhaps it

was because we were on our own, with a simple, independent aim. And although now in the midst of a most savage storm, we still felt in complete control of our destinies.

What mountain shall we climb today? That's difficult. But once the decision is made the rest is tactics, and one can be happy struggling with tactics. Every mountaineer loves planning the route, the places to bivouac, the logistics of what to take. One feels freed from the abstract and unsolvable and returned to the real and important. The aim is so beautifully clear. You can even see it.

The great joy this gives runs right through Bonington's writings. He is as egocentric as anyone and hates failure, but even failure is bearable if it leaves opportunities for a primitive struggle with a clear objective. 'As a youngster I was very keen on model soldiers and that has grown into an enthusiasm for war gaming', he wrote recently. Something of this enthusiasm contributes to his love of climbing. On the North-East Ridge of Everest in 1982 he was forced to admit that he was not as strong as his companions Boardman and Tasker, both twenty years younger, that he had no real chance of climbing the route, and that the only sensible solution was for him to accept a support role. And the most useful support he could give was to set up a camp on the North Col of Everest to act as the key to Boardman and Tasker's descent and a possible escape route. It wasn't a question of giving moral support from base camp but of doing something physical which made a direct contribution. And with that, the pleasure he derives from his mountaineering life returned:

> I was not depressed by my own failure and was even relieved that I had made the decision to withdraw from the summit bid. . . . I felt a vast relief of tension and actually looked forward with anticipation to our trip to the North Col. This was something which seemed a useful contribution to the expedition, was within my capabilities, and a goal in itself.

There was still a useful challenge to go for, with all the criteria – immediacy, danger, decisions – of 'serious play'.

However, it is the mountain explorers who really exemplify the longing for a kind of re-found primitivism in mountaineering, and who tell most clearly of the joy it can give.

The doyen of early twentieth century British explorers is Dr Tom Longstaff. 'One can still see in the mind's eye the slight figure, jutting beard, keen eye, strong graceful hands and ever youthful spirit', remembers Peter Lloyd. When Longstaff confessed his ambitions to be an explorer to his father, he advised him to take a medical degree; 'every man, he said, ought to have a profession to fall back on'. Longstaff did so, but never lost his interest in adventure and exploration, and as well as being a mountain explorer, climber and surveyor was a noted seaman, making hazardous journeys to Spitzbergen and Greenland.

However much he enjoyed climbing, the pull of unknown territory was always irresistible to Longstaff. When he first went to the Himalaya in 1905 it was with the intention of attempting Trisul, one of the highest peaks in India. Then suddenly, and quite

Tom Longstaff, photographed by his sister Katherine Wedgewood above Arolla in the *Valais*, Switzerland, in 1904, the year before his first trip to the Himalaya and his attempt on Gurla Mandata.
(Photo courtesy of Mrs Sally Amos.)

Right: 'Living in the present'; Tom Longstaff's philosophy and sheer zest for life make him one of the most attractive as well as one of the most important characters in British mountaineering history. As Tom Patey, his doctor, commented: 'Some men never grow old. Age, after all, is no more than a state of mind. . . . The climbing world will remember Longstaff as the greatest mountain explorer of his time: those of us who knew him more intimately will remember him as one who had discovered the elixir of life.' (Obituary notice, *The Alpine Journal*, Vol 69 (1964).)
(Photo of A.O. Wheeler and Longstaff in Western Canada in 1910 courtesy of The Alpine Club.)

unexpectedly, he was presented with the rare opportunity of travelling to Tibet. 'What a chance! My plans for a mountaineering expedition would change into the prospect of a walk of some thousand miles across and round the Himalaya.' He couldn't resist it, though he did find the time to make a spirited attempt on Gurla Mandata, an important summit on the Tibet-Indian border, on the way. His team set a speed record by descending 3000 feet in 'a minute or two' in an avalanche. They all survived.

In the early decades of the twentieth century the mountains of the Indian Himalaya were particularly attractive territory for British explorers. They fell within the British administered territories of Kumaon and Garhwal; they are much closer to Delhi than the Karakoram; and Kumaon and Garwhal are amongst the most beautiful regions on earth. Longstaff returned here in 1907 and succeeded on Trisul, which at almost 23,500ft became the highest peak yet climbed. True to form, the ascent was made at great speed, Longstaff, a Ghurka soldier and two alpine guides he had brought from Italy reaching the top in June using what Longstaff called his 'rush tactics'; they climbed the last 6000ft of the mountain in one ten hour push and then descended 7000ft to their camp in the next three. It was an impressive performance, which owed much to the fact that the whole party had been at over 15,000ft for most of the previous month and were therefore very well acclimatised. Shades of Messner's recent performances.

Like all great mountaineers, Longstaff had an eye for the future. He had seen and noted Changabang, the mountain which three quarters of a century later was to be at the forefront of technical Himalayan climbing when Boardman and Tasker climbed its West Face. In fact he was to print a photograph of the West Face in his autobiography. He must have sensed that a mountain of such appalling beauty – its most obvious comparison is with Cerro Torre in southern Patagonia – was destined to play a significant role one day; 'a sheet of palest granite draped with vast icicles, one a thousand feet long. In some ways this was the most amazing mountain I have ever seen'.

Longstaff's mantle was in due course taken over by Eric Shipton and Bill Tilman, the two men who between them were to dominate Himalayan exploration in the 1930s. Like all explorers, Shipton and Tilman craved the freedom of the exploring life. Longstaff was apt to say that Everest in particular was a millstone round mountaineers' necks, and that the sooner it was out of the way the better. Shipton and Tilman felt much the same. All that grandiose rhetoric put forward so interminably by Sir Francis Younghusband and others – the glorification of man, his preparation for loftier living and so on – once the mountain was climbed it could all be put aside and one could at last concentrate on simply enjoying oneself.

Of the two, Shipton is the more immediately attractive character. He was the son of a Ceylon tea planter, but neither made nor inherited much money and was short of funds throughout his life. He eked out a living as a lecturer and writer and during the Second World War served as British Consul in Kashgar. The post-war period was a difficult one for Shipton. Although he led the Everest reconnaissance which climbed the Khumbu

H. W. (Bill) Tilman (1898–1978) cooking pemmican at camp VI (3450ft), during the traverse of Bylot Island, Canadian Arctic, July 1963. Many of Tilman's sailing-cum-mountaineering expeditions were extremely bold and he eschewed rescue facilities – such as two-way radio – to a degree few people do today. This insistence on self-reliance was not pig-headedness or even pride, but a philosophical principle. 'Every herring should hang by its own tail', as the proverb has it.
(Photo: Bruce Reid.)

ice-fall in 1951 and the hugely successful (in terms of mountain exploration) Cho Oyu expedition of 1952, he was ousted from the leadership of the '53 Everest expedition, divorced in the mid '50s, and to regain his spiritual equilibrium spent several years as a forestry labourer in Shropshire before enjoying a second concentrated period of exploration in South America in the 1960s. Shipton made some difficult climbs, most notably perhaps the West Ridge of Mt Kenya with Tilman, but it is as the archetypal romantic explorer, searching for something inward of which the mountain is only a symbol, that he is rightly remembered.

Tilman, born two years before the turn of the century, was ten years older and fought in both world wars. In the 20s and early 30s he planted coffee in Kenya, where he first met Shipton. When he returned to England he resolved to devote the remainder of his life to exploration and adventure, though shortly afterwards he fell from a climb in the Lake District and seriously damaged his back; he was told he would never climb again. Tilman inherited family money, never married and was a self-sufficient individualist, as demonstrated by a comment recorded by Jim Perrin: 'I've had my peccadilloes, but the trouble with women is, they get in the damned way'. Like Longstaff, he was attracted not only to mountains but to all wild places, and in the second half of his life became as distinguished in the field of adventurous ocean sailing as he already was in mountaineering. He could be brusque and reserved and as a sailor was notorious for driving his crews hard. (A famous advertisement in *The Times* read: 'Hands wanted for long voyage in small boat; no pay, no prospects, not much pleasure'.) At the age of 79 he disappeared sailing whilst on an expedition in the South Atlantic.

In 1934 Shipton and Tilman applied their energies to Nanda Devi, the highest peak in the Indian Himalaya. Standing at the centre of a great ring of mountains which block off almost all lines of approach, Nanda Devi is strikingly beautiful and has the extra allure of inaccessibility. Longstaff himself had tried to reach it, and he was by no means the first. They did not succeed in climbing it – Tilman did so with Noel Odell as part of a British/American expedition two years later – but they did reach its base, and the '34 venture has come to enjoy a very special place in mountaineering history, standing as a glorious example of the small, informal, expedition philosophy for which Shipton and Tilman retained a deep preference all their lives, echoed in Tilman's much quoted view that if an expedition cannot be organised on the back of an envelope in half an hour it isn't worth organising at all. It is a view which can never fail to appeal to our sympathies, and when Tilman made a rare appearance at a British mountaineering conference in the late 1970s (not the sort of event he had a natural sympathy with), he stole the show.

So what is the explorer's special reward? Little-visited areas have a timelessness, a sense of being part of another era, which the Tilmans and Shiptons of this world crave. I was reminded of this on a recent visit to the Kurdopin Glacier in the West Karakoram. The Kurdopin was first visited by two Dutch explorers, Philip Visser and Jenny Visser-Hooft, who made several Himalayan journeys in the 1920s and '30s, bringing

The author and Duncan Tunstall (foreground) climbing through spindrift avalanches and storm towards the summit of the Kurdopin pass, central Karakoram, 1987. Shipton had reached the pass in 1939, only to be prevented from exploring its northern side by the outbreak of war.

Bonington wrote of a storm on the Eiger: 'There was an odd sort of enjoyment about the entire venture. Perhaps it was because we were on our own, with a simple independent aim.' I felt similarly about this adventure. *(Photo: Stephen Venables.)*

guides from Europe. On the Kurdopin they were eventually stopped by a considerable ice-fall and forced to retreat. Descending the side of this ice-fall half a century later I was delighted to come across two superbly made stone cairns. Who had built them? No hunters would come so high. I like to think the Vissers' party left them to mark their high point. Sitting by them, the first human sign for many days and so unexpected, put time and timelessness into a new perspective.*

Later, below the ice-fell, we escaped thankfully from the tottering blocks of ice and descended the glacier's brown moraines in the late evening sun. We needed water, and ahead could see a likely spot; below a mountain ravine a scree fan, dotted with gorse and grass, spread out and blocked the path. And then movement: before we could make out their shapes a dozen large animals fled the horizon. They were Himalayan goats, Ibex, *markhor* – something of the sort. How I longed to see them close! One day, when I'm too old for climbing, this is what I'll do; come here, to the high scorched pastures below the snowline and sit in a mountain eyrie with the silence and the longest lens a man can buy, waiting, waiting, until the rare inhabitants of these places, those most private and magical lives, reveal themselves. Diemberger's crystals? These also are they, elusive and rare, fleeting moments which cannot be told.

Whether any of this is an accurate reflection of real primitive peoples is questionable of course. Having recognised that contemporary civilisation is missing something, it is all too easy to idealise primitivism and create a false image of the noble savage, a silly romanticism in which nature is the only good. But a more immediate way of living is certainly possible and, rightly or wrongly, primitive peoples and their lifestyle stand as our symbol of it. When the Italian mountaineer Fosco Moraini visited the villages of the Kalash Kafirs of Afghanistan in the 1950s he felt he was witnessing a scene 'eloquent of fundamental realities'. There seemed to be a wisdom embodied in the life of the Kalash which a more sophisticated urban society had lost. It is to be regained only by intentional culture shocks which force us to question our assumptions, and life in the mountains, essentially the life of the vagabond, is one way of doing that. More generally, travel – not package tour travel but 'real' travel – can return one to a sense of fundamental things.

During a round-the-world motor-cycle trip the middle-aged Ted Simon found himself in Thailand, overwhelmed by 'the change that has taken place in our perceptions of life and death . . . It began to seem quite extraordinary to me that in the western world a person could, and probably would, go through life without ever witnessing death, let alone viewing a naked corpse . . . I could not bring myself to believe that this was

---

*There is a traditional belief that the female share in early Himalayan exploration was particularly formidable. It is a view that the classic literature has hardly discouraged. Mrs Visser-Hooft, for example, owned a pet Tibetan mastiff, a breed famed for its ferociousness, which, according to her account of their travels, she took for walks on a lead. (See *Among the Kara-korum Glaciers*, Edward Arnold, 1926).

Above: 'The flute player.' Woman of the Kalish Kafirs, Nuristan, at a time when, in Maraini's words, 'their world was still quite genuine and nearly untouched by foreign influences.'
(Photo: Fosco Maraini, 1959.)

Right: Fosco Maraini, aged 80, at home in Florence with his oriental library.
(Photo: Maraini collection, 1992.)

healthy'. Mountaineers are led to the same conclusion. Every climber is likely sooner or later either to see someone killed or get so close to it themselves that it makes them think. Anyone who is seriously involved in climbing in the greater ranges has a list of dead friends. And walkers too are apt to find that the primitivist nature of what they do invites thoughts about 'fundamental realities'. Food, warmth, shelter; where does it come from? Climate; how does it affect us? Suddenly we realise that in modern life we are indeed 'dangerously detached from the basic facts of existence', taking things for granted and never seeing them at first hand, only on TV screens.

So it is hardly surprising if some of those who have experienced the primitive life at first hand come to scorn modern comforts altogether, and despise the squeamish refusal of the rest of us to look the harshness of life in the face. There is a marvellous passage at the end of *A Short Walk in the Hindu Kush* when Eric Newby and his companion Hugh Carless come face to face with the almost fabled explorer Wilfrid Thesiger. Not quite Burton meeting Livingstone, because this is not a meeting of equals. Newby and Carless are essentially modern men, innocent but adventurous, returning to the primitive on a temporary basis only, just as most of us do. That is why *A Short Walk* falls within the scope of this book. Thesiger on the other hand is not returning to the primitive; in Newby's pen-portrait he *is* a primitive, though also the classic imperial Englishman. Over supper he tells them about his medical experiences:

> "Do you do it? Cutting off fingers?"
>   "Hundreds of them," he said dreamily, for it was very late. "Lord, yes. Why, the other day I took out an eye. I enjoyed that . . ."

The shock of the primitive, its different assumptions and its different modes of thought, makes one more critical of western ways, and there is much to be said for the view that if you don't come back thoughtful and uneasy from a climb in South America or a trek in Nepal the whole thing has been pointless. The money you spend, the western materialism you flaunt – if mountain tourism goes no deeper than that then it is a sad affair. Return to the primitive should make you a radical.

Death for example; perhaps our fear of it is not healthy after all, but a tool of repression? The fear of death can become a fear of life, so that instead of living we surround ourselves with endless safety regulations and do's and don'ts. Mountaineering as it is meant to be throws off regulations and the rewards of that, though they have to be paid for, are very real.

One way to talk about death is to do it humorously. The late Tom Patey was a master of black humour, and so was Don Whillans. Patey attempted the Eiger with Whillans, and wrote a classic portrait of the man:

> "Somebody's left a boot here," I shouted to Don.
> He pricked up his ears. "Look to see if there's a foot in it," he said.

Mountaineering is dangerous, though the dangers are generally less than public perception makes them. What is more widespread, and probably more insidious than literal tragedy, is the keener *sense* of death that it offers. And this, though exhilarating, has a danger of its own: it is liable to make a lot of modern life seem downright irrelevant. The triviality of everyday life, that key existentialist sentiment, is something mountaineering can make one feel deeply. On the return from any major mountaineering experience one's feelings are inevitably two-fold: on the credit side an exhilarating sense of living on a higher plane than normal, above trivialities; on the debit side the problem of learning to take those trivialities seriously once again. For however pointless earning a living, say, might seem when one is struggling for life in a blizzard, the person who cannot take everydayness seriously is in danger of going mad.

Re-adapting takes time, and is never easy. 'Even though Terry is the most understanding husband I could have, every time I go away we have problems with our relationship', wrote Julie Tullis. 'I am immediately plunged back into the routine of a housewife. The initial difficulty is that I do need time alone to come back from one world to the other, which appears very anti-social when I have been away for so long.'

These problems are only too common. Returning to everyday life, it is difficult to take anybody, or anything they are doing, seriously. A return to the primitive encourages a mental retrenchment in which forgotten elements of life regain their rightful status and the trivial things are seen for what they really are – trivial.

The root of it is a completely new sense of the physical life. Mountaineering is a sharp reminder that one is only flesh and blood, that in normal life we tend to forget the vulnerability of our bodies, forget that at its core life is about physical survival and that nothing else matters. Even when physical actions are serious, as in driving for example, we are generally unaware of it. But in the mountains or on a rock-climb we rely on physical prowess and are acutely aware of it. It is one more feature of the game which helps to 'graft us back into nature and a sense of reality regained'. Who are these people who say mountaineering is not real life but an escape? Up in the hills they seem like blind fools, and one is more inclined to question what is so 'real' about 'ordinary' life.

Yet in one sense return to the primitive is undeniably an escape. It is an escape from the individual ego.

The human ego is a burden as well as a pleasure; everyone is trying to get on, everyone is trying to be a success. The attraction of the primitive life is that it takes one away from these pressures which make it impossible to feel psychologically free. Most anthropologists agree that primitive peoples have a quite different sense of individuality from ourselves, being less obsessed with leaving their mark on the world, less afraid of death – and, as a result, more free.

But this does not mean that the primitive has no sense of self. Discussing Melville's *Moby Dick* the critic Michael Bell has pointed out that the peculiar advantages of the primitive mentality are summed up in the whaling ship's harpooner, Queequeg, whose 'unquestioning cosmic acceptance seems to give him an extraordinarily impersonal sense of his own existence'. He is truly an individual, yet believes deeply in some greater scheme of things which, because it is beyond his control, removes the more stressful aspects of egocentricity. He is both more and less egocentric than ourselves.

And really there is no contradiction here, for it is only by becoming fatalistic that one can break free from fear and actually concentrate on being oneself. Is there anything less inspiring, less individual, than modern man, obsessed by his own individuality? Is the answer to life really the avoidance of physical risk and continuing to live as long as medical science makes possible? The result is so often a poor sense of self spread ever more thinly. Yet the primitive radiates a sense of self which we envy.

The eastern concept of *dharma*, life's duty or purpose, throws some light on this. *Dharma* is a state of mind now largely alien to the West, and thus increasingly alien everywhere else too, but it still produces in some peoples a sense of identity and meaning out of all proportion to their material wealth. The shepherds of the Gaddi, migratory sheep and goat herders of the Kulu region of the Indian Himalaya, are able to explain an aspect of *dharma* which to us seems quite radical: that one's actions should not be determined by what seems logical or most efficient, but by what is traditional. Only in this way can one gain a sense of real purpose. The Gaddi travel constantly, with all the inconveniences and difficulties that implies, and to the western observer it is not clear that such constant upping of roots is really necessary. But that is to miss the point. Necessary or not,

> we are a shepherding people. We are in the habit of going with the flocks: it is because of the *dharma* that Lord Shiva gave us. It happened like this. The gods were making their way through the Himalayas. They came to a particularly high, snow-covered pass. They struggled to get over it but failed. In despair they sat down, tired and bad-tempered. Lord Shiva was the angriest . . . In a fury he took a pinch of dirt from his body and hurled it to the ground – out of his dirt sheep and goats were created. The flock walked across the snow and as they went they made a path. Then, following that path, the gods were able to cross the pass. In thanks Shivji (the familiar name for Lord Shiva) gave the Gaddis the privilege of looking after the flocks. But these days it is very difficult, so young men . . . are going into the army, government service, and shop-keeping. That's good, but it's not our *dharma*.

However fanciful they may seem to rational minds, such myths have a great power to order and make sense of life. Primitive peoples know quite well that they can be shot down in flames by rational argument, so if they are wise they take steps to prevent such argument taking place. That is why they will not tell their stories willingly.

Jung recognised this clearly. At one point in his life Jung spent some time with the Pueblo Indians of North America. He discovered that their religion was a form of sun worship. But it was a worship which the Pueblos believed influenced and was even essential to the sun itself; they believed that without their rituals the sun would quite simply be unable to cross the sky. 'I then realised', says Jung, 'on what the 'dignity', the

A porter rests on the long walk to the Kangshung Face of Everest, Tibet, in 1988.
(Photo: Stephen Venables.)

tranquil composure of the individual Indian, was founded. It springs from his being a son of the sun; his life is cosmologically meaningful, for he helps the father and preserver of all life in his daily rise and descent ... That man feels capable of formulating valid replies to the overpowering influence of God, and that he can render back something which is essential even to God, induces pride, for it raises the human individual to the dignity of a metaphysical factor'.

Well, we have lost that. We have been giving up the notion of cosmic significance since Copernicus gave us a rude awakening. And perhaps that contributes to our current obsession with our own individuality – what else is left?

But mountains offer us an alternative, because they present us with such a grand arena that we are almost bound to reflect on our personal insignificance. They have a sense of permanence and stillness which can be profoundly affecting. Once again, the result is to remind us of the narrowness of our everyday thoughts and concerns. 'It is this feeling of steadfastness of timelessness, imbuing every rock, that is such a comfort and so staunch a support in these days of outward change, of flux and uncertainty.'

This is the quality which underlies the fascination antique lands like Tibet or Bhutan still have for the western mind. A fine but depressing book about Tibet, *Land of the Snow Lion*, has recently been published by the mountaineer Elaine Brook. Like thousands before her, Brook goes in search of the mystic vision and its benefits, but whether it is the fault of the Chinese or the tourists they have let into the country, Tibet has changed, and the image that stays with one now is not of timeless wisdom but of surly Chinese bus drivers constantly looking at their watches. The country which for so long stood outside time has at last succumbed like everywhere else. In the Potala Palace in Lhasa a sad young monk, finding that Brook speaks Tibetan, gives her a book of Buddhist prayers. "Take it," he says with tears in his eyes. "It is finished here."

Aldous Huxley also has some interesting things to say on how to find a new outlook. Indeed Huxley has a more than passing interest for any study of mountaineering consciousness. He was deeply interested in how to raise man's awareness of life, and this is perhaps *the* central concern of mountaineering. In his utopian novel *Island* Huxley used rock-climbing as a tool for raising the awareness of the young. He wrote extensively on the visionary experience, and in *Heaven and Hell* talked of taking consciousness to those 'antipodes' of the mind of which we are normally unaware by invoking the power of static, as opposed to dynamic, objects.

> The sculptured figures of Egyptian Gods and god-kings, the Madonnas and Pantocrators of the Byzantine mosaics, the Bodhisattvas and Lohans of China, the seated Buddhas of Kymer, the steles and statues of Copan, the wooden idols of tropical Africa – these have one characteristic in common: a profound stillness. And it is precisely this which gives them their numinous quality, their power to transport the beholder out of the Old World of his everyday experience, far away, towards the visionary antipodes of the human psyche.

Mountains have that stillness. They encourage visionary thought and attract anyone looking for a sense of unchanging values.

> To whom the mountain stillness is a song
> More sweet and strong
> Than all by human art and rapture poured
> From voice or chord
> An ecstasy that thrills and fires the blood,
> Half understood . . .

But such states of mind are very fragile, and easily destroyed by the incursions of man. In discussing landscape painting, Huxley holds that though the inclusion of the human dimension may make a scene classically beautiful, it will certainly prevent its being visionary. To Huxley, visionary landscape can never mean 'the middle distance'; it can only mean the distant view or the close-up. The reason is that only these exorcise human involvement, leaving an emptiness and silence in which the mind can breathe and be transported towards its antipodes. The panoramic view can be visionary; so can the close-up, one's face pressed against a cliff, and Mummery realised this clearly a hundred years ago. But if the panorama includes a thousand fell-walkers, or the cliff cannot be seen for climbers clambering over the rocks like so many chameleons (to rephrase Patey), those visionary qualities will be lost.*

In mountains, less often on a roadside crag, the sheer power of the forces of nature are displayed to shame us into a little humility. Nowhere, not even on the sea, are their scale and uncaring nature seen to better effect. In the avalanche and the rock scar and the grinding of huge boulders along glacial torrents we gain a sense of change, but change which proceeds on its own time scale, inexorably, and oblivious to man and all his works. The mountain village, perched beneath a crag or in the alluvial fan where two rivers meet, seems to be there as a temporary favour. Surviving on a long lease, it will be uprooted in the end.

And in a mountain storm we know we are powerless. We are presented with forces beyond any sense of human powers and the result is both an exhilaration and a tremendous relief. It is a relief to realise there are forces greater than ourselves, and every mountaineer has taken pleasure in the battering rain, the wind howling, and the snow piling ever deeper against the door. If one feels safe one even takes pleasure in being out in such weather, in feeling its force and observing its magnificence. Most of us feel better for rubbing faces with nature in the raw, partly because it is all good exercise, more fundamentally because it takes us out of ourselves. Compare this with 'normal' life, in which nothing demonstrates

---

*'This is all very different from the South Col! you can remark crisply, as you watch bikini-clad girls swarming over the rocks like chameleons.' From a peerless article, *The Art of Climbing Down Gracefully*, in *Mountain 16* (1971) and *One Man's Mountains*.

our separation from nature more graphically than our inability to accept its tantrums. We think weather patterns are there just for our benefit, and are absurdly affronted when trains grind to a halt and cars get stuck in snowdrifts.

Many of these ideas can be summed up in the concept of 'natural piety'. Natural piety is the core characteristic of the primitive mentality, and quite rightly has a religious connotation, for nature is indeed sacred. It is infinitely more powerful than we are, and beyond our comprehension. In some sense it is to be worshipped, propitiated, looked up to. And one is bound to wonder whether the religious life of mountain peoples is ever really the result of dogma, and not always an intuitive reaction to the natural world. Mountain peoples are in general remarkably stoical, and this characteristic is reflected in their religions. God will provide, Allah is all-powerful; such sentiments are ideally suited to people living in mountains. The concept of a deity who is all-powerful and who always knows what is for the best reflects perfectly the attitude they have to adopt, whether they like it or not.

But whilst for primitive peoples natural piety is both real and convincing, for us it can be only a feeling. Primitives are animists and see nature personified in Gods who have a more or less human character and need to be kept sweet. The trouble for us is that we cannot accept such ideas *unless* we keep them vague; they are altogether too fantastic. We have to avoid an overtly religious interpretation, and the result is that there are many people today who welcome the feeling of natural piety and are attracted to mountains because of it, but who nevertheless regard themselves as atheists.

Natural piety is a kind of cosmic ecology. Ecology is the science which stresses the interdependence of all living things and teaches that if you tamper with nature the effects will ripple through the system and be more far-reaching than you expect. Ecology as we know it is hard-headed science, but its principles and emotional content can clearly be extended so that it includes not only living things but all objects in the world, so that the interdependence is not only physical but spiritual. Byron expresses it when he writes:

> I live not in myself, but I become
> portion of that around me; and to me
> high mountains are a feeling, but the hum
> of human cities torture; I can see
> nothing to loathe in nature, save to be
> a link reluctant in a fleshly chain,
> class'd among creatures, when the soul can flee
> and with the sky, the peak, the heaving plain
> of ocean, or the stars, mingle, and not in vain.

We all of us have had our 'moments', and surely many of them have been just this: a sudden realisation of being a part of a whole. At such times the present moment is heightened yet we feel simultaneously bound up with the past. Ritual helps that, so ritual is

'There is . . . something uplifting, something ritual, about an old camping ground deep in Himalayan country. . . .' Base Camp at Bularung summer pasture, Kunyang Kish expedition, 1980. *(Photo: Dave Wilkinson.)*

The route to Muktinath on the Annapurna circuit, northern Nepal. Mountain scenery is determined not by political boundaries but by geology and climate. Here in the rain-shadow of the Annapurna massif the panorama is reminiscent not, as in so much of Nepal, of Switzerland, but of the stark beauty of Pakistan and the Karakoram. *(Photo: Mary Bartlett.)*

central to anything felt to have a spiritual component, including mountaineering. The finding of a camp, more likely than not in a place where others have camped before you, all the elements of domesticity and the making of a meal which at home seem such a chore, ensuring one is as comfortable as possible, then lying out in a sleeping bag and watching the stars and a vast silence – that familiar routine can take on a deep joy.

But as with visionary landscape, to be successful it requires the avoidance of other people and the facilities man-in-the-mass invariably demands. There is nothing spiritually uplifting about approaching a modern alpine hut for example, though such places have other advantages. There is, on the other hand, something uplifting, something ritual, about an old camping ground deep in Himalayan country, about making oneself at home in old sheep pens and collecting water from a stream where men have done the same for centuries.

Is this sentimental? Surely not; the sense of 'rightness regained' is genuine and deeply felt. It would be sentimental to expect primitive peoples to keep living like that just to please us, but there is nothing sentimental about returning to do it ourselves on a temporary basis. To admit to having lost something is not to deny our other advantages, and what we have lost is '. . . an absolute authenticity of environment, a sense of the past in the present, a complete identification between people and place . . .' It is the mode of living central to all the classic mountain explorers, who tell us that wild country is an inspiration in a way that nothing else is because it encourages a sense of harmony between the environment and the individual, the feeling that one is but a part of something greater. It is this which brings those moments of sheer delight, and it is unspoilt country rather than technical climbing which is the key to it. 'I now felt myself to be on terms of intimacy with this wild region which, to my mind, is the highest reward of any mountaineering venture', wrote Shipton of his very un-technical explorations in Tierra del Fuego. Natural piety was the lasting reward of such activities, whatever the pure excitement at the time.

It is also the reward of mountain walking. Natural piety is the philosophical idea which comes over most strongly in modern writings by walkers and backpackers, where it is made perfectly clear that natural piety is more complex than a simple appreciation of nice views, and that its roots go deeper than aesthetics. Two hundred years ago Wordsworth was saying much the same thing.

One of the things we have to do when we walk or climb is be rhythmic. The rhythms cannot be chosen by us but must be attuned to the environment and one feels, however irrationally, that there is a connection between rhythmic grace and the primitive mentality. The beauty in movement of primitive peoples, whether it be the dance of tribesmen in Africa or a Hindu woman walking, walking, across the dust of India, stands in stark contrast to the bustle of any modern city. We are put to shame by our gracelessness.

The world's children, young or old, run up hills with excitement and flop down exhausted after a couple of hundred yards, but those with experience of the hills let the terrain dictate the pace and in so doing demonstrate an involuntary respect for the land. One does it to avoid wasting energy, but it then emerges that there are other, unexpected, rewards. Efficient movement over the land, neither too fast nor too slow, promotes a sense of peace and makes one feel closer to the natural world. This is quite unconscious, but it does develop an unmistakable sense of 'rightness'. And I suspect that many of the nostalgic feelings for the past which are there in every generation of mountain writing are in fact sincere attempts to explain this deep feeling, attempts which have simply gone wrong. All that comes over is a sense of bitterness and dislike of progress, when what was intended was a plea for the importance of rhythm. That such attempts do go wrong is not surprising. Rhythm must attune itself to the land and by its very nature it avoids the most extreme situations. On its own, therefore, it rarely accomplishes anything new, and is in constant danger of deteriorating into the boring and the mediocre. The backwoodsmen's appeals to 'the old days' are almost inevitably uninspiring; we are more inclined to remember desperate struggles on climbs at the absolute limits of our ability, occasions when there may not have been much rhythm evident but at least we achieved something.

The difference is reflected in our aesthetic reactions. Someone struggling and about to fall off is very exciting to watch – exciting rather than aesthetically pleasurable. We are given a sense of fighting nature, of conquering it. Movement over the land which is neither too fast nor too slow on the other hand, or graceful and controlled movement up a difficult rock face – these things are a pleasure to watch, but they are not exciting.

There is a peculiar feeling of well-being to be gained from rhythmic, economical movements. It is a sensation open to anyone who enjoys watching their feet moving neatly, and many mountaineers have felt they would continue to climb 'even if there was no view and no technical difficulty, nothing except the simple movement upwards'. It is a satisfaction which can be found in all forms of mountaineering, though solo rock-climbing, in which the climber carries with him nothing but his own body, it perhaps the closest of all to a pure celebration of human physique and the exhilaration of muscle and co-ordination used to the full. At no time has this been truer than today when the aesthetic element in rock-climbing is reflected in colour co-ordinated clothing and full-blown narcissism.

Not that the 'rules' of aesthetic style need be constant. Not so long ago the received wisdom in rock-climbing was that one's weight should be on the feet not the arms, with three points of contact with the rock at all times. That was the static or 'old school' style of climbing, perhaps best summed up in the principle that one should be capable of climbing down anything one has climbed up. I was first taken climbing at the age of eight or nine by one of the few full-time professionals of the old school, Jim Cameron. Jim lived in the Lake District and carried on working with his regular clients until well into his 70s. I had a few days' climbing with him every summer for a number of years, and every year the question on my mind was the same: would we at last forsake the boring old routes on Shepherd's Crag we had done a hundred times, and at last go somewhere exciting? We never did; and perhaps it was a good thing. Jim's equipment was rudimentary and he still used shoulder belays. Neither his equipment nor his philosophy encouraged one to discover one's limits.

My unsatisfied longing to see into new worlds led to great frustration. But there were compensations. Jim knew all the routes he used like the back of his hand and what I remember about his climbing, apart from his obvious love of it, is rhythm. Everything was in control, everything was pleasing to see. He never grabbed but moved smoothly, his nailed boots balanced on minute holds he had used a thousand times.

Progress has put the static style in the museum. Strong arms are indispensable to today's hard climbs; no-one would expect you to climb down, and even to climb up an element of premeditated 'uncontrol' may be necessary. But none of this has altered the importance of rhythm, and today's experts are every bit as aesthetically pleasing as their predecessors.

But rhythm is more than an aesthetic titillation, or simply the best way to improve your climbing standard, and what makes it so is its mental effects. Mountaineers have found that physical harmony (of rhythmic movement) has a knock-on effect in promoting a mental harmony (of natural piety). There is no need to 'do' anything, least of all think anything; just be rhythmic, and a new perspective develops of its own accord. It is in many ways a more comforting perspective than we are used to, and it explains why increasing numbers of people are forsaking the Sunday papers and going out for a walk in the hills instead.

These ideas crop up continually in Winthrop Young's writings. For Young, climbing is 'the supreme opportunity for perfect motion', and the knock-on mental effect is never in doubt.

'A striking figure with the appearance and culture sophistication of the highly cultivated late Victorian intellectual', Geoffrey Winthrop Young was both the shaping personality of rock-climbing in North Wales at the beginning of the century and a superb Alpinist. A polymathic figure, he avoided falling into the trap which now lessens the standing of so many other once-prestigious climbers: blind conservatism. He accepted change, and he sympathised with youth's ambitions. Perhaps it was the unusual breadth of his experience which enabled him to do this. He was proposed for membership of the Alpine Club by Sir Alfred Wills himself, yet he knew Joe Brown, the most important figure in post-war British rock-climbing.

In the years leading up to 1914 Young was pushing forward the technical standards of Alpine climbing much as Mummery had done a couple of decades earlier. The ascent of the South Face of the Täschhorn in Switzerland by Young, V. J. E. Ryan and the guides Franz and Joseph Lochmatter and Joseph Knubel (Franz Lochmatter was later to accompany the Vissers to the Karakoram), was an astonishing performance; the hardest alpine rock-climb of its time and still one of the most serious of its kind. The way Young scrambled and heaved, using every trick he could think of to get up the thing, including his teeth, while the Lochmatters pulled on the rope for all they were worth and all five of them

A view of Scafell, perhaps England's finest mountain, with the rocks of Broad Stand down which Coleridge descended on 5 August 1802 rising from high on the shadowed slopes on the left. From a distance the terrain looks innocuous, but on a wet day, and particularly in descent, it is awkward, exposed and dangerous. *(Photo: Doug Scott.)*

'He never grabbed but moved smoothly, his nailed boots balanced on minute holds he had used a thousand times.' Jim Cameron, one of the last of the old school, on Jack's Rake, Pavey Ark, Langdale, in his late 60s. *(Photo: author's collection, early 1960s.)*

wondered whether they would ever escape (our chances are 'about one in five' announced Young after some consideration) – all this has helped to produce a classic adventure story out of what was certainly the era's major feat.

On the outbreak of war Young served at Ypres as a non-combatant and then in northern Italy. In 1917 he was seriously wounded and subsequently lost his left leg, a particularly cruel fate for someone whose delight in life was based so deeply on masterly physical movement. It altered the mountaineering game fundamentally for him, but perhaps because of that produced his most important writing.

Young was to return to the Alps after the war with the same outlook and the same ambitions he had always had: to celebrate his physical prowess and so gain a feeling of exhilaration, a 'delight of rhythm that may reach almost to ecstasy . . .' For the first few years he refused to believe he could not recapture it, even though the result was full of frustration, by contrast with what had gone before, a nightmare. But finally he was forced to admit that the old prowess was no longer there, and that the comparison of the present with the pre-war years was too painful.

> This was not the least like the sort of luxurious, rapturous transfiguration, with the rhythm of movement still tingling in the muscles and the song of life humming through the silence in one's ears, which had surrounded such high moments in the past.

What was wrong? The trouble was that he was no longer 'in tune' with the mountains. There is in them a rhythm and a wholeness, and to be truly satisfying one's mountaineering, whether easy or difficult, walking or climbing, has to produce a rhythm of its own which reflects that. Looked at in this light the root of the problem was obvious: difficult climbing with one leg was an utterly unnatural and unrhythmic thing to do, so far from bringing one into a closer mental contact with the natural world it merely underlined one's separateness. It was mountaineering undertaken purely as a challenge, to prove one could do it, and this could never again deliver the real delight of the game. The key to happiness now was above all things to feel that one was 'obeying laws of movement and of living inspiration which have correspondence with the same principles on a deeper plane of existence'. In fact Young was to claim that that had been the real root of it even when he was at the forefront of difficult climbing. A new route, achievement; these had been secondary even then to a sense of harmony. And harmony would always imply matching one's ambitions to one's abilities.

> It was made clear to me that neither in the mountain nor in myself had the virtue of my mountaineering lain; but only in the relationship which could be created, and constantly renewed between us; and that this, on my side, depended upon the technique of climbing . . . I had lost the secure technique which greater Alpine mountaineering demanded, and I had become dependent upon sheer effort, and the technique of others. Further, owing to the excessive call I had to make upon physique alone, I could no longer bring the wholeness of myself, observation, thought, apperception, into natural contact with the completeness and

'Geoffrey, how do I write a book in six weeks?' John Hunt taking advice from Geoffrey Winthrop Young outside the Pen-y-Gwryd Hotel after the successful Everest expedition in 1953. Young (1876–1958) was the undisputed elder statesman of British mountaineering after the war, as well as being a notable man of letters – his prose and poetry is aesthetically and meticulously formed – and a distinguished educationalist. His Easter gatherings in Wales in the years before and immediately following the first world war are traditionally regarded as the apogee of civilised mountaineering; a time when action and imagination came together. As well as the leading climbers of the day, guests included luminaries such as Aldous Huxley, Ernest Rutherford and Charles Darwin. *(Photo courtesy of The Alpine Club.)*

G. W. Young, Percy Farrar (an outstanding Alpinist at the turn of the century), Bishop Evans, P. Dickerson and George Leigh Mallory (1886–1924) at Pen-y-Pass, during one of Young's exclusive Easter meets. Mallory's sensitivity and grace delighted Young. He had 'a strikingly beautiful face. Its shape, its delicately cut features, especially the rather large, heavily lashed, thoughtful eyes, were extraordinarily suggestive of a Botticelli Madonna, even when he had ceased to be a boy – though any suspicion of effeminacy was completely banished by obvious proofs of physical energy and strength.' (R. L. G. Irving in an obituary notice in *The Alpine Journal*, Vol XXXVI (1924).) *(Photo by Marcus Heywood, courtesy of The Alpine Club.)*

complications of great mountains. The right balanced relationship therefore never came into being between us at all; and the confident joy that belonged only to the right relationship could never follow.

There could be only one conclusion: he must learn to be content with less demanding mountaineering. But once he saw that, and accepted that is was not what one achieved that mattered but the matching of ambition and ability, he had solved the problem. No amount of determination could make up for the mismatch and make hard climbing pleasurable again, but by turning to fell-walking, which is what he did for the rest of his life, he re-established harmony and his pleasure was as great as ever. 'We discover that there are degrees of mountaineering difficulty which can be associated productively with every stage of our altering energy.' That the gentler approach of later years can be every bit as fine as the one glorious hour of youth is wisdom. But without the sort of crisis Young experienced, it is a wisdom which is easy to ignore.

Mountains teach us to accept natural rhythms rather than fight against them. Such rhythms are amongst the 'fundamental realities' of which Maraini spoke; they are elements of natural law. In wild country we are aware of the seasons: mountain rivers in spate in the spring as glaciers melt; the race against time to grow crops in high mountain valleys before the onset of winter; above all the harsh contrast between summer sun and winter's cold. And it seems to be only in wild country and among primitive peoples that we can accept the cycle of birth and death. Primitive life encourages an attitude to the individual's death more stoical and accepting than our own, because the natural world has impressed on the primitive something from which modern man is divorced; the primacy of the rhythmic process, not only inevitable but 'right'.

There is more to mountaineering than this of course, because mountaineering is also expansionism, and expansionism by its very nature is trying to transcend our individual mortality, to transcend our personal unimportance. When someone dies in the mountains one would have to be very cold-hearted to feel it was 'right'. Inevitably, one wonders about potential that will never be realised, achievements and pleasures that can never now come to fruition. Yet there *is* a sense in which one accepts more readily because of the environment, because of return to the primitive. Most mountaineers, I think, would rather see a close friend, or even themselves, killed in the mountains than in a car crash, even though the result is exactly the same.

The nomadic life-style has a part to play in this too. One thinks of Conway, walking through the Alps from end to end and arguing passionately that the true pleasure of mountaineering is to be an ex-centrist. (Not an 'eccentric' but an ex-centrist, someone who doesn't stay in one centre but travels around.) Crag-climbers are not nomads, but explorers are, and so are backpackers and Himalayan trekkers.

Are human beings nomadic animals? It is possible to see the nomadic urge not only as proof of our wish to expand, but equally as a way in which we can forget for a while our individual mortality and the hopelessness of trying to escape from it. In any event, temporary nomadism is endlessly attractive. Longstaff explained why:

> Since happiness is most often met by those who have learned to live in every moment of the present, none has such prodigal opportunities of attaining that art as the traveller. Every day as he moves or halts there is something new to enjoy. At every evening's camp is the charm of taking possession of some new home. Attainment of a set objective is but a secondary matter; the traveller should not anticipate the journey's end. So long as he loses consciousness of self and is aware in all his senses of the present scene, almost any part of the world is as good as another. Mountain or desert, it is all one. We shall have realised ourselves as being a tiny portion of the universe; not lords of it.

This sums up certain aspects of the mountaineer's return to the primitive and reminds us that whilst it is very different to the expansion into new worlds with which I began this book, it is not simply the reverse of it. If one of the rewards of expansionism is a heightened sense of existing, of being alive, of being important, the same is true of return to the primitive. Once again, the effect of raw nature, more powerful and magnificent than humanity in every way, is not to deny us a feeling of significance but to confirm it.

The difference between the two is not so much to do with whether humanity is important but whether the *individual* is important. Expansion gives us a sense of self as individuals; it is ego-confirming. The power of a return to the primitive is also to give a sense of self, but without a belief in individual importance. Life in general, yes; me in particular, no. The search for a personal uniqueness is always a struggle, and when we speak of going to the hills to find peace, to escape the rat-race, to work off frustrations and *get away*, what we are trying to get away from is the pressure to be recognised – in short, to be significant as isolated individuals. The mountains comfort us, because under their influence we realise that it doesn't matter. 'Life', in some generalised sense, will carry on. The individual life will not. And in natural piety one's sense of place in the universe is not in spite of that fact but is founded on it.

'Less than a mile from our base camp I was in paradise, . . .' Porters climbing the hillside above the
south bank of the Baltoro Glacier, central Karakoram, Pakistan.
(Photo: John Cleare.)

5 Fusion in Diversity

In *Many people come looking, looking . . .* the American mountaineer Galen Rowell describes trekking up the Baltoro Glacier in Pakistan *en route* to the Trango Towers. After several days' bad weather the rain clears and he sets off for a walk, delighting in the clean air and wild flowers. Suddenly he comes across the tracks of a snow leopard, rarest and most elusive of Himalayan animals, and turns uphill to follow it. The tracks become mingled with those of an ibex; the leopard is following its prey. Eventually the tracks peter out on the side of an impassable ravine, and Rowell stops:

> I had the feeling that I was being watched. The leopard may have seen me while tracking the ibex, and dodged into the ravine where it could hide under the overhangs. I sat down on a boulder and looked for movement. There was none. Less than a mile from our Base Camp I was in paradise, even if the leopard never showed itself. Clouds were lifting from the higher peaks, exposing Concordia and the Gasherbrum peaks in the sunset light. The pursuit of the leopard had temporarily locked me into the present where I entered a state of optimistic expectation about my involvement with the natural world.

Rowell's experience seems to me to demonstrate something which is found in so many of the best moments, the moments which we take away with us and treasure: a meeting of opposites which transcends logic and is too profound ever to communicate fully. In this case it is a new sense of time, of timelessness within the present moment. And this is what makes mountaineering more than a sport, more serious than cricket or golf. It brings together opposites, things paradoxical and logically irreconcilable, and is thus an echo of human life in a much wider context.

To claim, as mountaineering does, that a willingness to die is a necessary condition of a worthwhile life, is to recognise a profound truth. More generally, if we ask which is more central to mountain experience – the exhilaration of physical achievement or the insight of oneness, the quiet ecstasy of the nature mystic – we are driven to the conclusion that the question itself is mistaken. The core of the thing lies in the realisation that the sum is greater than the parts. For not only can physical achievement and mystic insight occur together; the one may even promote the other. This is one of the areas in which Doug Scott has written well. Half way up the 3000ft of bare granite of the Salathé Wall in Yosemite Valley, California, he rubs noses with, of all things, a frog:

> How many more were there, I wondered. Perhaps enough to fill a ten-foot square box. Then he hopped away into the rock, so perfectly camouflaged that I couldn't spot him again. I felt really good up there because of that frog; he seemed to show that we were all in it together – not just the El Cap scene, but the whole business of being alive.

With paradox so deeply ingrained it is hardly surprising that the real joy is so often to be found in the travelling, not the arriving. On Broad Peak the whole weight of his reason forced Diemberger to say: 'Yes, it was all over. I had been up there. It was the climax of a climbing-life – it was the Thing itself . . .' But underneath he knows quite well that it wasn't the Thing itself at all. If it had been he would have stopped climbing. The thing itself can never end. 'If only it could be perceived' wrote Hornbein. But to have a goal – the summit – is to live in tension with the promise of final revelation, whereas to arrive there is to destroy the tension and realise that the tension *was* the revelation.

The root of it is that most fundamental of human problems, the reconciliation of the finite and the infinite. And the depth of mountaineering is not to find an explicit solution, but to live through the problem.

Thus it is the tension between finite and infinite which informs that dry and at first sight least important of subjects, climbing ethics. What technical aids are permissible on a climb? Our equipment is now so good that if no limits are imposed then everything becomes possible. But when everything becomes possible, everything becomes pointless. In his article *Murder of the Impossible*, Reinhold Messner argues vehemently against the use of bolts in mountaineering. 'Do not destroy the dragon!' he warns. For our ancestors the dragon was a living monster who inhabited the mountains and threw down anyone who sought to destroy the infinite. Today he is the 'impossible' route, the route which given the necessary equipment is not really impossible at all. We *can* throw him down, reduce him to a mere logistical exercise. With bolts, the blankest walls can be climbed.

Messner claims that such routes are wrong, and though the argument is partly aesthetic, at a deeper level it derives not from aesthetics but from a wish to preserve the infinite. Without the infinite there can be no tension between logical opposites and without the tension there can be no inner satisfaction. The secret is not to subdue the infinite to the role of vanquished enemy but to feel finite and infinite complementing each other, and that is why in mountaineering thought no mountains are ever 'conquered' and anyone with a real love of them dislikes such terms.

The idea of a balance is at the very centre of mountain experience and makes itself felt in endless discussions about the equipment one is allowed to use on different routes, the pros and cons of large and small expeditions, and the delicate balance to be maintained between risk and security. On the one hand is the spirit of adventure, the urge to be bold and to commit oneself. On the other, the wish to cover one's retreat, to offset dangers and to make life more comfortable. And there is no final 'answer' to any of this. Its outward aspect is always changing, and improvements in equipment (for example), are always offset either by bigger objectives or by bolder climbing styles.

Mountaineers invent their own rules; no-one imposes them. And they invent them because experience has shown that this is the only way to make mountaineering satisfying. Ethics are only symbolic of a profound dualism, and of the realisation that if either finite or infinite is lost the game is destroyed. Conversely, it is when both are present to the correct degree that it attains its greatest heights. What is a classic route? No-one has ever been able to quite say, though it is possible to recognise both classic walks and classic climbs. Perhaps it is a route which symbolises balance.

The tension between finite and infinite certainly underlies mountaineers' ambivalence towards success. Success is a two-edged sword, fulfilling ambition but destroying a symbol of infinity, so there can be a very real relief in failure. 'How can I help rejoicing in the yet undimmed splendour, the undiminished glory, the unconquered supremacy of Mount Everest?' wrote Mallory the year before he disappeared on the mountain. Such sentiments may be illogical but they are heartfelt and sincere, and they make of Mallory a tragic as well as an heroic figure.

George Leigh Mallory has been immortalised like no other British mountaineer except, perhaps, Whymper. He was educated at public school and Cambridge; he was good-looking – even beautiful – and charming; and he disappeared with one companion close, perhaps very close, to the summit of the world. But however heroic the image, the truth is that although Mallory was ambitious he was also confused and a terrible prevaricator, and it was really the play of fate as much as strength of purpose which determined his involvement with Everest. He could never really decide whether he wanted to go on the expeditions or not, and was constantly on the point of backing out. Tibet he regarded as 'a hateful country inhabited by hateful people', and as for Everest:

> I sometimes think of this expedition as a fraud from beginning to end, invented by the wild enthusiasm of one man, Younghusband; puffed up by the would-be wisdom of certain pundits of the A.C.; . . . our present job is to rub our noses against the impossible in such a way as to persuade mankind that some noble heroism has failed once again.

Longstaff regarded him as 'a very good stout-hearted baby, but quite unfit to be placed in charge of anything, including himself'.

But nowhere is the inner paradox more clearly demonstrated than in the need to preserve the 'untouchable', an idea which invites a religious interpretation as 'the sacred'. The concept is found in all forms of mountaineering and in every social *milieu*, and it is genuine and important, even though it is always overwhelmed in the end by the inexorable drive to achieve what can be achieved.* It is the idea of the untouchable which lies at the root of the dismal meeting of East and West which can often be observed in Himalayan countries today. The Norwegian philosopher Arne Naess tells an

---

*Paul Ross, a Lake District activist of the 1960s, has related how he once set out to solo *Kipling Groove* in Langdale, a route put up by the much-admired Arthur Dolphin and at the time widely regarded as the hardest climb in the Lakes. He was called back by his companion, Pete Greenwood. ' "Come back down," he said. . . . "What's up?" I said. "That's Arthur's route and if you solo it, you'll ruin it." So that was that. He had a tremendous respect for Dolphin.'

interesting story of egging on the Sherpas who live below Gauri Sankar in Nepal to demand a ban on climbing the mountain. Gauri Sankar, or Tserigma, is a very striking peak and was once thought to be the highest mountain in the world. To the Sherpas it is sacred; that is, it is a representation of the infinite to which mere humanity should not presume to reach.

> When we suggested to the Sherpas of Beding, beneath Tserigma, that they perhaps might like to have its fabulous peaks protected from 'conquests' and big expeditions, they responded with enthusiasm. A special meeting was announced, and the families voted unanimously to ask the central authorities in Kathmandu to refuse permission for climbing expeditions to Tserigma. ... The sherpas would not mind 'losing' the money they could earn from expeditions ...

For the Sherpas there was a moral point: it is wrong to seek to reach the infinite. Modern western thought takes a different view of the infinite, and thus of the mountain too; it is simply something else to be overcome. For us morality is not involved – it is merely a question of practicality. If we retreat it is not because reaching the summit is wrong but because it is too hard, or too dangerous, or we have agreed to respect others' feelings. We are always ready to return if things begin to look more hopeful.

And yet ... and yet an uneasiness remains within us. Of course mountaineers do not spend their time theorising on the balancing of the finite and the infinite; of course the sort of system-building with which this book is concerned hardly ever appears on a rock face, during a walk over rolling hills, or at Camp 6 on Everest. There, one has left abstruse matters far behind and one's concerns are refreshingly real. But such questions still inform our minds on an unconscious level. The whole strength of mountaineering is that simple motives can bring sophisticated rewards. Questions of balance and opposing factors are not always there explicitly but they are always there beneath, underpinning what we do. We are tired of trying to find explicit solutions and failing, but by experiencing these things and living them out it may be possible to come to an implicit solution, an understanding which can never be satisfactorily explained or defined but which is real because it is experienced.

Sometimes, it is true, we are made consciously aware of the underlying dualism through first-hand experiences, ideas, or even symbols. Howard Somervell tells an interesting story from the 1924 Everest expedition. Before Mallory and Irvine made their final, fated attempt on the summit, he and Norton were out in front, and camped at 26,800 feet – 'a bit too low, but still – we had done 2,000 feet a day with ease up to now; and there was little more than 2,000 feet left for the morrow' – were all set for an attempt on the summit. They were to reach over 28,000 feet before retreating. 'I remember a curious sensation while up at this camp', Somervell wrote later: 'as if we were getting near the edge of a field with a wall all round it – a high, insuperable wall. The field was human capacity, the wall human limitations. The field, I remember, was a bright and uniform green, and we were walking towards the edge – very near the

Theodore Howard Somervell (1890–1975) in the 1960s. Somervell was an outstanding polymath: surgeon, musician, mountaineer and of course artist – many of the pictures of the Tibetan landscape he made during the 1922 and 1924 Everest expeditions are superb, despite being executed on brown packing paper, the only thing he had to hand. On Everest his culture and width of accomplishment created a natural bond with Mallory. Later, he devoted many years of his life to work as a medical missionary. *(Photo: Diadem Archive.)*

Wilfrid Noyce (1917–1962), photographed on Everest in May 1953. Noyce has been called 'the last of the poet-mountaineers' – a classic error of mountaineering nostalgia, no more accurate than Bonatti's claim that Messner was the last of the great romantics. Noyce was killed climbing in the Pamirs with the great Scottish pioneer, Robin Smith. *(Photo courtesy Mrs Rosemary Ballard, formerly Mrs Rosemary Noyce.)*

edge now, where the whitish-grey wall said: "Thus far, and no farther." This almost concrete sense of being near the limit of endurance was new to me, and though I have often felt the presence of a Companion on the mountains who is not in our earthly party of climbers, I have only on this single occasion had this definite vision of limitation.'

It is when the finite and the infinite are both strong that mountaineering seems intuitively 'right'. And it is when the balance is lost that we feel uneasy. Out-and-out conservatism which worships the past and hates new trends should be rejected, but we should be equally uneasy when the lure of the infinite takes over. That is the lasting significance of the tragic summer on K2 in 1986, when thirteen people died in a number of separate accidents, giving the world's second highest mountain a reputation to equal that of Nanga Parbat in the 1930s. One might argue that with the mountain festooned with climbers in quite unprecedented numbers, statistics almost guaranteed accidents. But the K2 tragedy indicates more than that. It reminds us that the correct balance between finite and infinite – ambition and acceptance, ego and humility, call it what you will – a balance which is a very personal thing and hard to find even at the best of times, is yet harder when there are external complications. It is a sobering reminder that even the most experienced mountaineers may be thrown off balance by sponsors or the presence of too many other people.

This is one reason why crowds are anathema to the mountaineering spirit. A lasting satisfaction is only to be found by creating a relationship between oneself and the environment, what for Young was a form of romantic trust; in balancing one's urge to do, to discover, with the finiteness of the human position in the world. It can be expressed in different ways, but however you say it, the crux is to reconcile opposites, and to do that successfully requires one to forget other people, for their example only confuses the issue. Instead of concentrating on oneself, as one ought, one falls back into comparisons with others. You have to be something of a genius not to.

Which brings to mind Don Whillans. Whillans was one of the finest all-round mountaineers of the post-war era; a brilliant rock-climber in his day, a leading Alpinist, and a formidable performer in the Himalaya. Yet Whillans' achievements, though impressive, have never really been sufficient to explain his deep and continuing influence. As a Himalayan climber in particular Whillans had a lot of failures, and in the last dozen years of his life he did little climbing. Yet his importance never waned. I believe the reason is that everyone recognised in Whillans someone who had faced the problem of maintaining a balance and solved it. It was not that his particular solution was 'right'; what is right for one is wrong for another. But he stood as a symbol; someone who had seen the infinite and not had his head turned by it. He looked the part too – the dour, beer-drinking Lancastrian with the flat cap who had seen it all before and remained with his feet firmly on the ground, impossible to impress.

Donald Desbrow Whillans (1933–1985) is for 'insiders', if not the general public, the most influential of post-war British mountaineers. He was 'awesome – literally' (John Barry); 'a very small man with a slow Lancashire voice, . . . and a direct, blue-eyed look, almost innocent you might say but very direct so that it would be hard to get away with anything undetected. . . .' (Wilfrid Noyce in *To the Unknown Mountain*); in his later years 'an institution' (Dennis Gray). He climbed very widely, but is seen here in what ultimately seems the most appropriate setting – gritstone country.
(Photo of Whillans on Heptonstall Moor, Yorkshire/Lancashire border in the early 1980s by John Cleare.)

Dougal Haston (1940–1977) on the North Face of the Eiger, March 1968.
(Photo: John Cleare.)

Many of mountaineering's paradoxes stem from the twin strands of expansionism and return to the primitive. A stronger sense of self for example has not only an expansionist element, the urge to do and achieve as individuals, but simultaneously a primitivist element which negates the individual and frees us from its anguish. This dual nature is well demonstrated by explorers who return from far-flung lands full of stories of being humbled by the beauty, scale and wisdom of the natural world. Homespun philosophies on the dangers of human intervention in the upspoilt corners of the globe follow. Yet it is generally clear that a substantial part of the joy of venturing into such places derives not from being there, but from the sense of self-importance which comes from getting there before anyone else.

Again, mountaineering brings together different forms of freedom: romantic freedom, the simple image of being able to do what one wants; and existential freedom, the freedom of doing the one thing, the only thing. The first is an element of expansionism, of the unceasing drive to become one's own master; the second of return to the primitive, in which the individual does not aspire to rule but accepts a more humble role within a greater scheme.

There are other examples. The meeting of danger and security; of what is new within a framework of living which is primitive and full of ritual; of asceticism and a refreshed appreciation of luxury. English Romanticism discovered that terror could be delicious, and by putting together two sensations which seemed paradoxical came nearer to the root of mountain experience than any rational explanation. The terror felt by mountaineers is both a physical terror and a mental terror of the unknown. Yet it is delicious, for we long to expand.

So it seems absolutely right that two hundred years after Gray we find paradox to be central to the experience of Chris Bonington, by far the best known British mountaineer and very much a public *persona*. In several autobiographical volumes the problem of reconciling the finite and the infinite is retold again and again.

On a mundane level Bonington is a highly efficient opportunist and tireless competitor. But this is true of most people who are successful. More interestingly, his writing makes it clear that security is absolutely vital to the thrill he finds in insecurity. Thus it is clear that he would never make a global hippy, forever on the move and without roots. Nor would he make a nature mystic. A Bonington divorced from civilisation, even a Bonington divorced from 'progress', which many outdoor lovers profess to hate, is inconceivable. Bonington is truly representative of his age, because he is forever jumping back and forth. Thirty years ago he escaped from a half-hearted attempt to lead a conventional life and build a career as a 'company man', and plunged into primitive living in the Patagonian Andes:

> The real thing about the night was the feel of it – the atmosphere. Eating because you want to eat, tearing the meat, held in greasy hands, with your teeth. Drinking when you want to, talking naturally, because you have something to say; listening because you are interested. This was a real enjoyment that went to the depth of my being.

Chris Bonington is now almost sixty, and for depth and sheer consistency his record is hard to beat. It is an irony for someone so much in the public eye that he doesn't photograph well, and most published pictures of him feed a public persona which is shallow and unconvincing.

Yet Chris, if one listens to what he actually says, is totally honest about the realities of what he does. In Brian Blessed's Everest book *The Turquoise Mountain* (Bloomsbury, 1991) he explodes at the author's cloying sentimentalism about mountaineering in general, about Mallory in particular – and by extension, about himself: 'It is crass nonsense to say that Mallory's attempt was noble! He was utterly and completely selfish! What you are saying makes me ill . . . He was selfish! Selfish! Selfish! . . . I am totally selfish too!'
(Photo of Bonington during the first ascent of Changabang, 1974, by Doug Scott.)

If Bonington had the makings of a global hippy in him he would at this point have declared he had found the answer. The freedom of the life; its honesty; the enjoyment it gives; what more could one want? But he is more complex than that. He wants the responsibilities of 'ordinary' life and he has what it takes to prosper in the modern world. He is not a self-employed businessman today simply through necessity; the life of the twentieth century achiever is as real and as important to him as the primitive life in tune with nature. In Patagonia he made the first ascent of the Central Tower of Paine with Don Whillans, part of a remarkable and continuing record of expedition success. But of the aftermath he wrote:

> It was a restless, disturbing period for me. Wendy and I had planned to wander up through the Americas after the expedition, spending the money I had made from climbing the North Wall of the Eiger. It had seemed an attractive scheme, but now my basic caution and need for stability began to affect me. I longed for solid roots, was worried about getting stuck into a new career and writing the book which had been commissioned just before I left England. I decided, therefore, to go back with the others rather than spend another six months travelling. Wendy was bitterly disappointed, for in many ways she is more adventurous than I. . . . It was largely meeting Wendy, and her contempt for traditional security, that gave me the courage to abandon a conventional career and plunge into the unknown; but a conflict between my desire for security and love of freedom remained. . . .

It is true that at the time he wrote this Bonington had little money, insecure prospects and a young family, but though his circumstances have since changed, his outlook has not. He still jumps back and forth as much as he ever did, and in so doing represents what is most typical of modern mountaineering – the manipulation, for the sake of intense experience, of contrast. He is satisfied with neither sophistication nor primitivism. He wants both.

Yet it is the very duality of the man which must make an insider's assessment of Bonington a mixed one. (The public have no such doubts; for them he is simply a 'success'.) On the one hand he is a first-rate mountaineer and a genuine enthusiast; on the other, his very approach seems a threat. Ironically, Bonington is in many ways a 'mountaineer's mountaineer'. He is ovewhelmingly keen, he is very good, and he would probably go on climbing if he was the last person in the world. No-one can sensibly suggest he climbs only for the money; anyone who derides his ability has simply not examined his record. But his very professionalism threatens what we love, so not everyone who criticises him can simply be dismissed as jealous. Those who question his record, yes; those who sneer at the money he makes, probably; but not those who dislike the publicity he encourages and uses so masterfully. Use of the media means money for expeditions, yet publicity is destructive, and inevitably so, of some of mountaineering's most cherished values.*

---

*Such a mixed assessment is not, of course, unique to Bonington. It has been a common view of many other professional mountaineers – Frank Smythe for example, a leading Alpine and Himalayan climber of the 1930s and another prolific writer.

The followers of Rousseau and the nature mystics are sure that of the two poles one is firmly superior to the other. The intuitive man is superior to the rationalist; a sense of oneness is superior to an isolated self; nature is superior to civilisation. And return to the primitive is superior to the responsibilities, the hypocrisy and the tortured satisfactions of modern life.

But mountaineering does not lead to that conclusion. Mountaineers often profess a simple romanticism, but they rarely act on it. They are aware of nature in a more complete sense than romantic sensibility can provide, because they take part in the drama of nature and see it more completely than anyone who relies on that unreliable master, imagination. The mountains of imagination, to use a phrase of the poet and climber Michael Roberts, are not the mountains of reality. The mountains of imagination are the mountains of the armchair enthusiast, and generally of those whose experience of mountains is not close. They are also the mountains of certain Romantic poets, for whom sentimentality is a virtue. The mountains of reality on the other hand are the mountains of the primitive, whose experience of them is too complete for sentiment. They are also the mountains of the mountaineer. And by the same token this book is not primarily about motivation, but about reward. What takes you to the mountains can be anything, for your motivation can be a false image, a fiction, as easily as it can be something real. There are an infinity of possible motives. Reward, on the other hand, springs from experiencing the mountains of reality, and these provide a much more limited range.

There is nothing wrong with sentimentality if we recognise its selective nature, but it becomes a distortion if we think it the whole picture. Some of the greatest Romantic poetry lays itself open to parody. Nature mysticism is not meant to be an idealisation of nature, and if it becomes that it deserves parody. It is meant to be a return to what is more real, not less; a return to 'fundamental realities'. And that presumably includes the evil as well as the good, the uncaring nature of mountains as well as their beauty.

Many people today feel that modern western living is incomplete. There is no need to attempt the impossible – an objective criticism of the way we live – in order to justify this. It is not such a radical statement. In fact if we remember our present distance from primitive living and how recent this is, it is almost a truism. Given the pace and scale of recent change and the contrasting slowness of genetic change within ourselves, modern life *must* be missing something.

Mountaineering is one way to redress the balance. Like Bonington, we move back and forth. Life is too secure; go to the Himalaya for three months. The land is too full of the signs of man; balance that with the stark and raw beauty of mountain wilderness. You feel caught in a system which controls your life and eats away at your self-respect; climb a rock face and feel gloriously renewed, confident that you can still 'do'. In all this, mountaineering is an escape from a world which seems one-sided.

And if one is escaping crowds, noise, the competitive society, one is escaping the dominance of certain ways of thought too. When Mummery wrote: 'I fear no contributions to science, or topography, or learning of any sort is to be found sandwiched in between the story of crags and seracs, of driving storm and perfect weather. To tell the truth I have only the vaguest idea about theodolites, and as for plane tables, their very name is an abomination!' he was objecting not to science so much as to the increasing dominance of its modes of thought. Mountaineering is meant to provide a balance to all that; so leave it behind when you go to the hills!

It is sometimes possible for opposites to be not just balanced but transcended, giving a sense of wholeness which only convinces one further that 'normality' is indeed incomplete. Such feelings of wholeness are the key to many of the intense moments of mountaineering. 'A recognition may begin to dawn that is neither totally alien and rationalistic nor totally 'oceanic' and mystically negated as a self, but includes both and goes beyond', writes Tom Lyon. That we cannot explain how or why this happens says more about the limitations of analytical thought that it does about mountaineering. The fact is, and we all know it from our own experience, *fusion is possible.*

New horizons tend to give a linear character to our experience of time. But time can also be circular, a characteristic associated with the primitive mentality, which is not concerned with the new but with things which in a sense are 'known all along'. And though we may experience one and then the other, mountain experience sometimes fuses them. The new is found in unexplored territory, in fresh panoramas, in the sheer uncertainty which is inseparable from mountaineering. As Messner puts it, what we want is 'long, hard days when we do not know in the morning what the evening will bring'. Yet underlying this are a range of rituals which are unchanging and which when combined with the visual impressions of mountain country widen one's perspective so as to make one think: nothing is ever really new. And this, I think, is something Longstaff had fundamentally in mind when he spoke of 'living in the present'. He did not mean what a superficial reading would suggest: a simple concentration on the present moment to the exclusion of all else. Longstaff's living in the present is not a narrowing of perception, a cutting off from the past and the future. It is precisely the reverse: a present so infused by a wider sense of time that it becomes living in eternity.

A similar feeling underlies Peter Boardman's description of climbing on the South-West Face of Everest, which he describes as 'dreamlike':

> The Face is a strange unreal world. All dressed up in one-piece oversuits and six layers on the feet, oxygen mask and goggles one seems distanced from where one is and what one is doing, like a sort of moonwalk ... This half-glimpsed quality was preserved far back in my mind. As a child I used to daydream over a painting in a big picture book, *Adventure of the World*, which depicted the tiny bold figures of Hillary and Tensing on the top of a summit that thrust out of a sea of clouds.

'As Pertemba and I crossed the traverse above the Rock Band in the early dawn of our summit day it felt as if we were on that highest peak above the clouds, as if the sight of the endless cloud sea was joining hands with the dreamland of the past.' The upper section of the Face, with the crux gully through the Rock Band and the upper traverse, clearly visible, peers above the ridge of Nuptse in this view taken from the south, close to the summit of Mt Mera. *(Photo: John Cleare.)*

As Pertemba and I crossed the traverse above the Rock Band in the early dawn of our summit day it felt as if we were on that highest peak above the clouds, as if the sight of the endless cloud sea was joining hands with the dreamland of the past.

Richard Frere wrote of the Cuillin Hills of Skye: 'The sight of those mountains was like looking at time; its power of evocation was so strong that it brought tears to my eyes, for it opened the book of memory at the right page and showed what was clearly in the margin . . .' Galen Rowell's thoughts on the hillside above the Baltoro make the same point: the urgency and shortness of the leopard's life combined with the eternal stillness of the mountains all around so that: 'less than a mile from our Base Camp I was in Paradise'.

And I remember on an expedition to Greenland racing alone for a final peak before the 'plane came for us, and being exhilarated not just by the situation but by the thoughts it created in my mind. What are we, we twentieth century men? Conquistadors truly, as Lionel Terray said; conquerors, ultimate egoists. We climb for the least inspiring of reasons, not to make peace with the universe but for something to do and for something to achieve. As for the summit, its greatest value is its simplicity. It is a reason for living so straightforward that even we fools can grasp it.

Yet this, thank God, is not the whole of it. Mountaineering is not really an invention of modern man at play. Always we have lived with these expressions of what is greater than ourselves, and always we have found the experience necessary. This is the intuitive understanding of all mountain peoples, for whom great mountains are sacred and climbing a pilgrimage or else a form of blasphemy. This is the real world, the world of fact, within which our personal ambitions are fantasies and can never be anything else, liable one day to dissolve like the mist in the wind.

Thinking so, I approached my peak, skis gliding silently across the snow. Nowhere have I felt so well the silence and desolation; nowhere have I felt so keenly my own ego. At its foot I took the skis off quickly and fitted crampons. In a landscape which had seen no-one since time began I was working to a schedule reckoned in minutes, playing a game only we could have invented, a game near-perfect for this being who cannot be satisfied with less than everything. The climb had only one section of any difficulty, a short slope of new windslab over hard ice. I climbed it quickly, listening fearfully for the sharp 'crack!' of avalanche and disaster. Like love and hate, triumph and tragedy were so like to each other in that moment. On the summit the snow lay in great sheets, shaped by the wind beneath a clear blue sky. A thin layer of powder moved over it, filling my tracks. Looking west the inland ice rose up in a great wave, unbroken at last; turning, I could make out black dots in the distance – camp, four miles away. I was two minutes ahead of schedule and listened with held breath for the hum of the aircraft, but there was nothing but the crunch of the snow crust as I moved my feet and the soft hiss of the powder. Later it would all deteriorate into farce, into self-indulgence and anything and everything that can go wrong with words, but for that

'Nowhere have I felt so well the silence and desolation; nowhere have I felt so keenly my own ego.' The final peak, soloed by the author on the final morning of the expedition, Kronprins Frederiks Bjerge, East Greenland, 1990. With its silence and its stark desert beauty, Greenland held me as the central Karakoram had done a decade earlier. *(Photo: author's collection.)*

The author in the Lemonsbjerge, East Greenland, 1992.
(Photo: David Stewart-Smith.)

brief time the moment was genuine, unsullied by sentiment, and I understood what Greene had felt of his own hazardous travels; it would have been so easy to be a saint.*

But ideas can be left aside, for movement alone has the power to fuse paradox. Tom Patey – one could use almost any climber as an example, but it is interesting to use Patey because he was not given to intellectualising climbing and was one of the best satirists the sport has produced – would have made humour out of the suggestion that there was anything symbolic about the way he climbed. Yet though he was not an elegant climber, and pooh-poohed the 'climbing is ballet' school of thought epitomised by Winthrop Young, he did have a remarkable ability to get up things. And because of that it automatically follows that from a mountaineer's point of view he had physical 'style'. In mountaineering, an aesthetic of movement cannot be divorced from its effectiveness. Young's joy in graceful movement is not wrong or inapplicable, but it is only part of the story. The core of mountaineering movement is something which goes beyond visual grace, something which combines it with a sense of urgency and plain old-fashioned efficiency. Patey had that combination and thus the 'right' physical style.

> The sort of climber I like to watch is the man who knows where he's going, and wastes no time getting there. A latent power and driving force carries him up pitches where no amount of dynamic posturing would do any good.

Are we Apes or Ballerinas? he asks, and answers: apes, definitely. But really we are both, and that includes himself.

The visual image can be superior to words. Words are always difficult. Poetry sometimes succeeds in transcending opposites, and so does humour. Humour is an important element in mountain writing, and not only because it enables us to talk about death without embarrassment or bad taste. But words will never wholly explain, and mountaineering is as good an example as any to remind us of their limitations. There is no substitute for experience, and Whymper's remark still applies:

> 'What is the use of going up mountains?' is a question which is often put.
> To such I would say: 'go up a good-sized mountain and you will know.'

---

*It seems fitting that even the way we explain mountain euphoria, Bourdillon's 'moments', should be rooted in approaches of almost total contrast. Soberly, we know that at times of high stress, and physical suffering particularly, the brain releases strong natural opiates, endorphins, on which the body can become hooked. (Or is it the opening of 'the doors of perception' which results from this release which is the real drug?) Less sober, more exciting, is the belief that when we are close to the natural world we may become attuned to 'the flow', natural energy streams, and that it is this inflow of energy rather than simply brain chemistry which explains the euphoria. Put another way, nature brings us close to the primal Creator and it is the Creator whose influence we then feel. One of the results of this kind of thinking is to make a distinction between primal wilderness and mere pretty countryside, the former now being seen as objectively superior, or at least more powerful. This has had an important influence on the conservation movement, from John Muir onwards. (See for example *Towards the Unknown Mountains* by Rob Wood, Ptarmigan Press, Canada, 1991.)

'Are we Apes or Ballerinas?' Tom Patey (1932–1970) remains one of the best-loved of Scottish mountaineers and one of the game's great satirical essayists.
(Photo: John Cleare, 2 January 1965.)

Notwithstanding stiff competition in the Himalaya, the Matterhorn remains the supreme mountain symbol of aspiration. Thousands, perhaps millions, have felt like Laurens Van der Post: 'I had been inflicted with a great longing to climb this mountain, which, to me, because of its shape and name was some sort of myth.' *(Jung and the story of our time, Penguin Books 1978, p.250).* The Matterhorn is also a timeless reminder that one must rub one's nose against a mountain to know how hard it is. As seen here, in the classic view from the north with Zermatt in the foreground, it appears formidable; but the Swiss ridge (facing camera) was the route of the first ascent and proved much easier than expected. Indeed, Whymper made some seven attempts from the Italian side before even trying the Swiss – on which he immediately succeeded.

(Photo by Friedrich von Martens, circa 1860, courtesy of The Alpine Club.)

6   The Religious Symbol

It may be controversial to claim that mountaineering has a religious significance, but that mountains do is universally accepted. Their visual form makes them natural symbols of religious aspiration. 'I will lift up mine eyes unto the hills, from whence cometh my help', sings the Psalmist. More than any other natural phenomenon, mountains suggest the soaring of the human spirit and its expansion into new worlds. 'It was no accident', claims Lunn, 'that the Gothic revival coincided with the new-found enthusiasm for mountain scenery. The trite comparison between a Gothic spire and an Alpine aiguille is not so shallow as it seems . . .'

Holy mountains are to be found almost everywhere, from Croagh Patrick in Ireland to Machapuchare in Nepal, but Mt Kailas, situated on the Indian/Tibetan border not far north of Gurla Mandata, is perhaps the single most important example. (When Longstaff approached Gurla Mandata in 1905 he did so via the traditional pilgrim route to Kailas.) Hindu and Buddhist mythologies have long made use of a symbolic mountain, Mt Meru, whose rivers are said to provide the life-giving waters of the earth. Four rivers are needed, to water the four quarters of the globe. It is a remarkable fact that four of Asia's great rivers – the Sutlej, the Bramaputra, the Indus and the Karnali – all rise in the region of Kailas, which has come to be regarded as the real-life Mt Meru.

Mountains have never stood for the church or for religious dogma so much as for the challenge of the individual's spiritual development. In other words they have stood for the esoteric (in the strict meaning of the word) tradition of spiritual evolution brought about by following a 'way'. Religious thought implies a belief in hierarchy, in good and evil, higher and lower, superior and inferior, and it is an obvious step to represent such spiritual differences by differences in altitude. Different parts of the mountain stand for different stages of development (exactly the same symbolism is found in Hindu and Buddhist temple architecture), the summit itself representing the goal, enlightenment, at which all aspects of the spiritual search converge.

This symbolism has been discussed by Marco Pallis, an active explorer and climber of the 1930s who was also a religious scholar. His book, *Peaks and Lamas*, recounts expeditions to the Gangotri and Kailas regions of India, Sikkim and Ladakh; the Gangotri, as well as being of religious significance as the source of the Ganges, has recently found renewed favour amongst climbers. But it is Pallis's subsequent book, *The Way and the Mountain*, which discusses the symbolism both of the summit and of the route to it, which is of greater interest here.

Any mountain possesses many routes, each starting from a different place and each having a different character and set of problems. Clearly, no-one can follow them all.

But that is not important. The important thing is to reach the top, and to do that one must choose a way; *one must make a commitment.* One must also have faith that the summit actually exists; it may not be visible at all the beginning of the climb. Pallis argues that in all these ways the mountain is an excellent symbol of the spiritual challenge facing man. He is not arguing that actually climbing mountains is a spiritual progress, but that the route to the top is a symbol of such a thing.

But though we may doubt the religious significance of MacIntyre on Shishapangma or Bonington on Everest, mountaineering in the wider sense certainly *can* have religious significance. For centuries mountains have formed the goal of religious pilgrimages and a pilgrimage is a physical activity, not a work of imagination. Croagh Patrick attracts many thousands of people every year, who climb to the summit, many of them barefoot, on the last Sunday in July. The difficulties to be faced on a pilgrimage to Kailas are considerably greater; hunger, passes blocked with snow, swollen rivers, bandits. To make it even harder the most devout proceed by performing *parikrama* – a technique of self-abasement and humility involving prostrating oneself on the ground repeatedly for the whole duration of the journey. On Kailas it takes fifteen to twenty days to get round the mountain in this way, compared to a normal walking time of two or three days. Judged from the state of mind in which religious pilgrimages are meant to be made, that extra two or three weeks is not wasted time, whilst attempting to complete the course in a single day, a feat known as *Chhokar*, is to be deplored. Practitioners of *Chhokar* are liable to find themselves dubbed *Khi-koor*, 'he who runs round like a dog'; clearly not complimentary.

Historically, harsh discipline and even the threat of death has often been regarded as central to pilgrimage. The Buddhist scholar John Snelling has pointed out that pilgrims were often dangled head downwards over precipices and left to die if they lagged behind. 'Clearly, the ultimate fears need to be invoked in order to bring about that pitch of seriousness that spiritual change requires.'

Religious pilgrimages still take place, though rarely with the sort of stringency once adopted as a matter of course. The modern 'pilgrim' is the western tourist; and can tourism ever be a serious religious affair? In *The Sacred Mountain* Snelling describes following the trek to Everest Base Camp in the early '70s. This was a modest enough undertaking, but Snelling feels it had religious significance for him. There were a number of well-defined stages – the seemingless endless crossing of forested valleys and ridges before one gets into the valley of the Dudh Kosi (most of this is now avoided by a road, built since Snelling was there); the Khumbu area of the Sherpa people and their main village, Namche Bazaar; and finally the high moraines above Base Camp from which the successful trekker can gaze up at the mountain – 'as solid and imperturbable as a great sage in deep meditation'. Snelling believes that it was exerting an attraction on him even during the walk's worst moments, and he was affected by the hardships, the effort that had to be made, and the dangers. He got lost

Above: Cairn and Mani stone at the entrance to the western valley of the circuit round Mt Kailas, Tibet. The southern aspect of Kailas, with its snowy summit, rises in the background.
(Photo: Sean Smith, 1987.)

Right: The imposing north face of Mt Kailas, photographed from the Tibetan plains by Tom Longstaff during his expedition to Tibet in 1905.
(Photo: courtesy of the Alpine Club.)

in the mist in the upper Khumbu, became rather frightened, and went to bed in a yak-herder's hut full of confused feelings and remorse at having 'trespassed upon the preserve of the Gods'.

It is easy to sneer at this little adventure and dismiss parallels between Snelling's three week holiday and the religious quest as fanciful and absurd. But mountain symbolism, when experienced in the flesh, is affecting. Trekking in the mountains can certainly lift the human spirit; who is to say it cannot teach religious truths?

Twenty years ago the Everest trek was already becoming overcrowded and at about the time that Snelling was walking there the American writer Peter Matthiessen was making for more remote areas of Nepal further west, where he was overtaken by that sense of vision which empty mountains inspire. His record of the expedition, *The Snow Leopard*, is deeply religious in tone. What does this mean? That mountains convey a sense of reality behind ordinary existence, and that we are normally 'asleep' to the fundamental things in life; but also that there are things greater than ourselves and that life requires the discipline of humility.

Mountains can humble us by making life dangerous. This is not something that is usually associated with walking, but Matthiessen's expedition is of the small, shoestring variety and is far from the tourist trail; under these circumstances '. . . the penalty for error makes me mindful as I walk among these mountains, heeding the echo of my step on the frozen earth'.

The root of Matthiessen's experiences, which are only half-communicable, an exploration of the inner mind, is that the mountains teach acceptance. Some time before the expedition began he had lost his wife from cancer, and his need to learn acceptance – of his wife's death, of everything – becomes symbolised in the leopard. *The Snow Leopard*; what is that? A rare Himalayan cat which few have seen or a symbol, like Diemberger's Alpine crystals? Well both, but also a lesson in acceptance. Matthiessen's book carries a drawing of this rarest of animals on the front cover, but in three months he failed to catch even a glimpse of one. Only the mountains and the old Lama of Shey Gompa who inhabits them can teach him wisdom: the acceptance of *what is*.

> Have you seen the snow leopard?
> No! Isn't that wonderful?

Not succeeding, which to us is failure, can only seem wonderful with a change in outlook. That can happen if one escapes the tyranny of passing time for a moment and feels instead that eternity is not in passing time but at right angles to it. *That* is the significance of Bourdillon's 'moments', of Raymnond Greene's *Moments of Being*, of Life is Now! The Buddhist traditions in which Matthiessen takes such an interest are forever telling him it is so but the Himalaya make him feel it too, the same feeling that Craig expressed about the British hills or Frere about the Cuillins. In such moments the transient is eternal and so its terror overcome. And unless we succeed in transcending that terror we will be back to Tom Lyon's fear, life as 'a desperate caricature of fear and grasping', in which, 'having in effect lost the whole world, nothing less than the whole world could suffice for security'.

Whether we are walking or climbing, mountains both comfort and inspire us. We are affected – uplifted – by them, and we firmly believe the effect to be a good one, though we cannot explain why. As the mountaineer and writer R.L.G. Irving put it, we have the conviction 'that in simply being among mountains and exercising our physical energies and our faculties of appreciation upon them we are moving along a road whose ultimate end is good'. And however objectionable it may be to our rational side, we cannot help feeling with Leslie Stephen:

> If I were to invent a new idolatry . . . I should prostrate myself, not before beast, or ocean, or sun, but before one of those gigantic masses to which, in spite of all reason, it is impossible not to attribute some shadowy personality.

Young's feeling of a romantic trust between himself and the hills represents something similar. In fact both Young and Stephen are responding as human beings have so often responded: with animism. Neither was a pantheist, but both felt more emotional reaction to high places than could reasonably be attached to mere lumps of stone.

Born in 1832, Leslie Stephen, tall and thin and forever smoking a pipe, was an important Victorian figure. There were early concerns for his health, which remained poor until he went to Cambridge where he took a mathematics degree. He became a Don and took holy orders, the academic life and a cleric's collar being more closely tied then than they are today, but eventually resigned his Fellowship because of religious doubts. He moved to London and began a distinguished career as a critic, editor and essayist. As editor of the *Cornhill* magazine he was influential in encouraging Robert Louis Stevenson, Thomas Hardy and Henry James amongst others. His own daughter was the novelist Virginia Woolf. He founded the *Dictionary of National Bibliography* and was its first editor.

But Stephen was also a leading light of the 'Golden Age' of Alpine climbing, perhaps the leading light. His record is certainly superior to Whymper's, and in the 1860s and '70s he crossed key alpine passes and made first ascents of several major peaks, particularly in Switzerland. The finest were the Schreckhorn – 'was there not some infinitesimal niche in history to be occupied by its successful assailant?' – and the Bietschorn, one of the most difficult high peaks in the Alps. Finally, in *The Playground of Europe* Stephen was to produce one of mountaineering's finest literary expressions.

Stephen's abandonment of his Fellowship and holy orders was a rejection of orthodox theology and the church, not an abandonment of religion. Being a man of religious temperament, he could never 'abandon' religion. But he did come to believe that religious seriousness and religious dogma were not the same thing. Failing to find spiritual satisfaction in the church of his day, he looked instead to mountains, and in this respect was no different from thousands of others before and since. On the other hand, the intellectual difficulties this created for him were considerable for a man of his background, and more worrying than we can easily appreciate today.

Stephen stands for religious experience, the most important aspect of mountaineering, the only thing which in the end can justify our taking it seriously. And though he wrote about them supremely well, he did not find the great 'moments' of mountain experience any more easily than anyone else. We might be tempted to think of the Alps in Stephen's day as virtually empty and therefore ideal for his purposes, but in his view they were already becoming too crowded and noisy, and in his later years he turned his thoughts increasingly to winter, when the whole region 'becomes part of a dreamland' and 'access might be attained to those lofty reveries in which the true mystic imagines time to be annihilated, and rises into beatific visions untroubled by the accidental and the temporary'.*

The English are often accused of being most reticent about the most important subjects – sex, politics, religion – and that was certainly true of many Victorians. The idea that mountaineering has a religious significance has never found easy acceptance among English writers and many of the mountaineers discussed in this book carefully avoided any direct reference to religion or religious experience. Yet their books show them to have been concerned with the great questions of time, reality, and intense living which are fundamentally religious questions. This was true of Stephen; it was also true, I think, of men like Shipton and Tilman. Theirs was a private search certainly, but then serious religious thought has never been much impressed by public relations. And this contributes to the unease with which mountaineering has traditionally looked on publicity and popularisation, as well as on any overtly religious interpretation.

Another problem, perhaps, is that religion suggests altogether too much seriousness, even fanaticism. When people object to a religious interpretation of mountaineering it may be this that they are really objecting to. 'Mountaineering is not a religion!' they say, meaning: 'it's only a pastime; don't take it so seriously'.

Still, this can be misleading. There is a persistent belief that British mountaineering has been moulded by gentlemen, who were gentlemen because they refused to take things seriously. But this is nonsense. It is true that there is a long and important tradition of eccentric amateurism, but it is wrong to think that this has ever excluded seriousness. In reality mountaineering has always been taken seriously, even fanatically, by the British as much as anyone else, and the real objection has not been against seriousness but against professionalism, efficiency and narrowness – different things altogether.

---

*Stephen walked in winter rather than climbed, though winter Alpine climbing was in fact well established by the end of the nineteenth century, and some remarkable feats had already been accomplished. It offered a new and undoubtedly exciting arena – but its early development is still surprising.

A third objection is against looseness of thought in a theological sense. Mountain mysticism is a widely-felt emotion, much expressed in mountaineering literature, but a mountain is presumably an inanimate object, whereas mysticism implies communion with an active power to which, of course, one then gives the name God. On this view, a mountain might conceivably be a symbol of God's power – it might be a Cathedral – but it is not, and never can be, God himself.

Leslie Stephen has often been accused of mistaking the altar for the deity. But Stephen (and this, apart from their elegant style, is what makes his writings important) was happy to admit the fault. To him, making distinctions between God, his symbol, and objects which encourage spiritual sensations, was not the important thing. What was important was not analysis but experience. The mountaineer who talks about religion is simply trying to express his feelings; he is talking in a tradition which tries to make religion human, not something for clever theological argument. Stephen knew, no one better, the intellectual arguments against 'mountain mysticism', but he was determined not to let arguments spoil his experience.

A similar view could be taken of animism, the attribution of a soul to every natural thing and phenomenon. Animism is a religious form which we associate primarily with primitive cultures, but that in itself does not make it irrelevant to modern times. We associate animism with the primitive in the same way that we associate Protestant theology with the West; it is primitivism's particular invention. But we ourselves are still archaic at root, we are still attracted by the 'shadowy personality' of the mountains, and if we defend the feeling it is because we are convinced of its value.

Most mountaineers, it seems to me, are existentialists by temperament. Consider, for example, the visionary power of mountains. Discounting trivial meanings of the word – unreal, vague, fantastic – we are left with the serious meaning: 'that there is another reality' behind this superficial work-a-day world, that the 'windows of perception' are occasionally opened for us, and that in such rare moments we *see*.

Now, that mountaineering can produce true visionary experiences is not in doubt. It is only their interpretation which causes discussion. So whilst Murray seems to interpret 'another reality' literally and writes:

> I came down from the summit filled with the acute awareness of an imminent revelation lost . . . Something underlying the world we saw had been withheld. The very skies had trembled with presentiment of the last reality; and we had not been worthy.

for David Craig the new reality is all in the mind, and his reaction to Murray:

> 'No, no, *no*,' I want to say to him. 'You *had* been worthy of the mountain, by being up there at all. *No* world was withheld; all there was to see, you saw.*

---

*Or as Victor Saunders expressed it more recently: 'There is no pot of gold, only the rainbow.' (*Elusive Summits*, part 4; Hodder and Stoughton, 1990).

But in answer to all this the reaction of most mountaineers is likely to be: does it matter? The value of mountaineering springs not from interpretation but from first-hand experience of the new and the unchanging. When McGlashan, a psychiatrist, calls his book *The Savage and Beautiful Country* he means the human mind. When Aldous Huxley refers to 'darkest Africas . . . unmapped Borneos and Amazonian Basins' he too means the human mind. But when Arnold Lunn, a mountaineer, speaks of 'The Undiscovered Country' we cannot be sure whether he means the human mind or the outside world, but suspect that he means both. And this is the faith that all mountaineers share and that all analysis must eventually return to: that action and imagination are connected; that we return to the hills to feel again that which we have forgotten; that the undiscovered country of the mountains gives access to the undiscovered country of the mind.†

A religious interpretation of mountain experience is encouraged by a change in the climate of western religious thought. It is often claimed that this change consists of a move away from our own Christian traditions towards a greater sympathy with the East, and there is certainly a great contemporary interest in eastern thought, not least among mountaineers. Doug Scott is a well-known example. It is also true that the mountain form and the mountain pilgrimage is more securely rooted in the religious symbolism of the East than it is in Christianity. But the important distinction is not between East and West but between the exoteric and esoteric religious traditions, between church dogma and religious experience. Many of the Victorians saw Christianity in dogmatic terms and to the extent that they enjoyed mountain mysticism themselves would have felt they were betraying their Christian faith. But the modern mountaineer can increasingly back up his claims to religious seriousness by appealing to more recent theological thought, to, say,

---

†Arnold Lunn, mountaineer, skier and religious thinker, was born in 1888 and educated at Oxford. His father was a Methodist minister and organiser of religious conferences aimed at church unity which took place in Switzerland. As a result he became a travel agent of some genius, creating the concept of winter ski resorts virtually single-handed. Arnold inherited both the theological idealism and the interest is skiing, gaining international recognition for the young sports of downhill and slalom skiing. He organised the first world skiing championships and introduced the new sport into the 1936 (Berlin) Olympics. He was introduced to mountaineering at an early age, but suffered an appalling accident when he was 21 when he fell from a route in North Wales. He was left with one leg three inches shorter than the other and more or less permanent pain for the rest of his life. In the war he was rejected for military service as unfit and served with The Friends' Ambulance Corps in France. His injuries did not curtail his mountaineering activities, however; he was a pioneer of ski-mountaineering and made the first ski ascents of the Dom and the Eiger. (How many mountaineers seem to have been unfit in one way of another! Frank Smythe was thought to have a bad heart, Mummery and Tilman weakness of the back. Willo Welzenbach, probably the greatest ice-climbing pioneer of the Alps, had a seriously weakened elbow. And so the list goes on . . .)

Lunn was also a thinker and Christian controversialist and at his best a superb essayist. His father brought him up a Methodist but he converted to Roman Catholicism in 1933 and by the time he died in 1974 had published over sixty books, of which sixteen were in the field of Christian apologetics, with titles like *Difficulties*, *Is Christianity true?* and *Is the Catholic Church anti-social?* His mountaineering books are indispensable literary sources.

James' *Varieties of Religious Experience*, or to contemporary Protestant theology in which experience, and private experience at that, takes the central role.

An important summary of the modern position has been provided by the Cambridge theologian Don Cupitt in *The Sea of Faith*, though as Cupitt is at pains to explain, his is not so much a theology as a new framework round which the individual must now build his own theology. 'Official' theologians of the future will be no different from the man in the street in this respect. Each of us must build his own system, and the results will all differ.

The beginning of the process is the abandonment of theological realism, the belief that the Bible or any of the figures in it are to be taken literally. Theological realism is the view which sees God as a Being sitting on a cloud or the parting of the waters of the Red Sea as an actual event. In the face of science, in the face of what Cupitt calls 'critical thinking', all that must be abandoned. Instead Christianity must become, as Christ's original message was all along, anthropocentric, the private search of each individual for his own salvation. What then become central are the facts, if one can discover them, of human nature; the psychological reality of how we are, not of how God is. God? He becomes 'the sum of our values', a symbol of human completeness or the way we would like to be. Heaven? Not a place but a state of consciousness. Hell? That too. Dogmas become 'expressive symbols of states of the soul'; the archetypal images proposed by Jung and others, aspects of God.

Which comes first, the theology or the experience? Often it has been the theology – otherwise how could we all agree on it? But in the 'new world' in which Cupitt claims we are now living and from which he says there is no return, the religious experience of the individual comes first and the theology follows from it. Theology becomes the creative act of each individual, a personal code which, as Cupitt freely admits, may be perilously close to a secular, as opposed to a religious, humanism. 'Religion is to theology as the performed symphony is to the musical score; a musical notation is doubtless a very clever invention and a most useful thing, but the score is after all only a set of instructions for performing the music'. The music is the important thing. So too in religion, religious experience is what matters and dogmas, laws, rituals and prayers are merely to get you there.

Cupitt ends his study with Wittgenstein, who came to see theology not as a justification or even an explanation of religion but as a symbolic way of expressing what is essentially inexpressible; religious experience. In *The Outsider*, Colin Wilson, who covers much of the same ground as Cupitt, though Cupitt's book is explicitly a book of religious theory and Wilson's a study of philosophical literature, ends with William Blake, who also put experience first and argument second. Blake was a *serious* religious figure. He was not interested in becoming Pope or Archbishop of Canterbury. His primary concern was not even with social values like justice or giving one's worldly goods to the poor. He was concerned with visionary experience, with trying to express it in words and pictures, and in laying down the way to obtain it. And this last is the vital point. What is of real interest is *method*, not interpretation or even expression. Blake's answer? That the individual must shake free from the trivialities which prevent his seeing anything worthwhile.

Mountaineers take the same view. Experience and how to obtain it is more important than trying to express or explain it. In mountaineering either you reflect on nature – the gentler illumination – or nature provides the sort of horrifying experience that forces the mind awake and *makes* you think. But in both cases, mountain becomes God. 'The fear of God'; of course God must be fearful, even cruel, otherwise no-one would take Him seriously or listen to what He had to say. We would all remain 'asleep'. Any God worth the name must be capable of being gentle or terrifying or anything in between depending on what one needs. Mountains can be all of those.

Mountaineering intellectuals have argued strongly against looseness of thought, and quite rightly. An anthropocentric view of Christianity is no excuse for that. But we are more likely to be sympathetic to the 'mystical' mountain writer if we realise that these key experiences are probably impossible to express accurately in words, and the writer's intention is simply to remind us that they exist. It is easy to find mystical writing which is vague, but what do we expect: a clear statement of the religious experience? In any case, it is very difficult to separate out one's own stylistic prejudices. Frank Smythe's writing is full of 'sublimity', 'the mountain vision', and various other undefined vague feelings, all of which can become irritating, and one is inclined to agree with Lunn: he was at his best as an interpreter of mountain adventures and at his weakest when he attempted to construct a religion from them. But he sold a lot of books. Murray's 'The very skies had trembled with presentiment of the last reality; and we had not been worthy' is by no means untypical of his writing and might be thought too ornate for modern tastes, yet *Mountaineering in Scotland* is universally regarded as a classic. Winthrop Young also can be sentimental, his style studied. Even the greatest of the Romantic poets miss the mark on occasion. It is man reaching for the moon, and no-one can do that unfailingly. The great are those who manage it at all.

What is important in mountain writing is not to conform to a given style but to convey one's experiences and emotions to the reader, and few would dispute the claim that the experiences and emotions that mountaineering provides are often religious in kind. What *is* a mistake, however, is to then build explicit intellectual beliefs around them on the basis of sentiment. For example, it is all too easy to allow a feeling of 'oneness with the surroundings' – genuine experience – to develop into the view that the natural world is innocent, more specifically that those who live close to nature are innocent. People who are in touch with nature are often unaware of much of what goes on in the outside world, but to suppose that this makes them innocent is absurd. Are the Pathans of the north-west frontier innocent? Clearly not. Some of them are bloodthirsty schemers. *They are also more religiously serious than many of today's law-abiding Christians.* A closeness to nature, and that includes the return to the primitive of the modern mountaineer, has a serious religious aspect at the same time that it lacks any moral aspect.

Part of the problem is that the West's Romanticism is not primarily religious; it is primarily an intellectual movement and a movement in art. In due course we abandoned our medieval prejudices and expanded our view of beauty to include the mountains in all their moods. We came to love both the picturesque mountains and the sublime. But love is an emotion, not an intellectual decision, and how is the emotion to be interpreted? In mountains one often feels oneself to be part of a greater whole, in worship in the presence of the sacred, yet western theology does not dovetail well with this. Popular Christian thought has generally put 'God highest, man below God, and nature a poor third'. It still has no bulk of substantial theological thought with which to buttress the mountain aesthetic. And the inevitable result is that the love of mountains begets all sorts of vague mystical philosophies, well-sprinkled with notions of pantheism and nature worship, rather than a serious and codified mountain ethic.

Eastern thought would seem to be more happily placed in this respect. Formidable philosophies of man's place in nature – in it, not over it – existed in the East well before the birth of Christ. Here, the picturesque and the sublime are deep in religious thought about man, his nature, and his place in the world, whereas in the West our delight in picture postcard scenery is liable to be only an aesthetic and as a result perilously shallow.

And mountaineering literature reflects these difficulties. There is plenty of religious feeling in it but it is vague and it is difficult to know what it means. We hardly have the language for it; we certainly do not have an agreed structure of thought. There is no tradition on which an author can base himself, knowing that his readers share it. All they share is his wish for such a thing.

Both the truths and the pitfalls of a religious interpretation are illuminated for us by Sir Francis Edward Younghusband, soldier and Himalayan explorer. Younghusband came from a notable military family in Northumberland and after an education in England entered the service of Empire in India in 1882. He could easily have carved out a safe and comfortable colonial career in which drill and the social niceties of the officers' mess were the major excitements, but the era of political intrigue and frontier manoeuvering with Imperial Russia, the so-called 'Great Game', was at its height, and a service career also offered unique opportunities to lead an exciting and outlandish life on India's frontiers and beyond. Within a few years Younghusband had made a number of impressive journeys, following in the footsteps of his equally adventurous uncle, Robert Barkley Shaw. Between 1886 and 1887, at the age of twenty-three, he travelled through Central Asia from Peking to Sinkiang, crossing the Gobi desert and continuing over the Karakoram into British India by a new route. He had soon made a name for himself as an explorer and political agent of great promise, with a rare ability to deal with recalcitrant local tribes and fly the flag. And he did it with that unique mixture of courage and confident superiority which was then regarded as the mark of the Englishman at his best. By 1893, at the age of thirty, he had become the first political agent in Chitral, and his career as a member of the ruling establishment seemed assured.

In Chitral, Younghusband struck up a friendship with George Curzon, soon to become Viceroy of India. Both men had strong views on the 'Tibetan problem', and regarded official British policy as weak and indecisive. So in 1903, when with many misgivings the British government finally sanctioned a military expedition into the country, Curzon (now Viceroy), chose Younghusband to lead it.

Few would regard the Tibet Frontier Commission as one of the happiest episodes of British foreign policy, and it marked a turning point in Younghusband's life. Though justified by the claim that the Tibetans were not keeping to their trade and frontier agreements with British India, its real reason was Curzon's belief, shared by Younghusband, that Russian influence in Tibet was dangerously escalating and needed to be countered. In any event, Younghusband marched on Tibet and eventually occupied Lhasa, a temporary incursion which made no difference to Russian policy and only helped the Chinese. The Tibetan army's equipment and organisation were medieval and both Britain and Tibet wished to avoid bloodshed, but inevitably there were military clashes, and equally inevitably the Tibetans were slaughtered on each occasion. Britain ended up with a good deal of guilt and a treaty which within a few years was largely irrelevant.

The whole western world, perhaps, now feels guilty about Tibet. The country's isolation, the Shangri-la quality of its capital, Lhasa, the harsh yet magnificent scenery, most of all an esoteric and little-understood religious tradition: all have combined to give it a romantic appeal which is unique. Yet the outcome has not been a happy one. Whatever may be the Tibetans' faults, and no doubt they are as great as those of any other peoples, T.S. Blakeney summed up the source of our guilt when he wrote that '. . . in at least one respect they were superior to almost all other races; they did not covet other people's lands, they only asked to be left alone. And when they were overrun, the world did not lift a finger to help them'.

With a change of government Younghusband became the scapegoat of Curzon's now discredited policy and was more or less pensioned off as British Resident in Kashmir. Historians are generally agreed that he was badly treated, and in part this was no more than political bad luck; Curzon had been replaced, and Younghusband was Curzon's man. But perhaps there were other reasons too. Younghusband, like any self-respecting mountaineer, was an individualist, and there is no doubt that he took policy into his own hands at times and altered it as he thought fit. This is something we can still admire in Younghusband today, even if some of his other characteristics and views seem dated. Like all of us he was a product of his time and upbringing, but his love of freedom and of running his own show, his being at times bloody-minded and taking foolhardy risks, makes him 'one of us'.

Of course, this is perilous territory. Any suggestion that all mountaineers have certain

Above: Mountaineer and orientalist Marco Pallis – who did not like to be photographed – in the Gangotri, Kumaun Himalaya, India, 1933.
(Charles Warren Archive, The Alpine Club.)

Right: The Tibetan Frontier Commission under Francis Younghusband entering Lhasa in 1904. The Potala Palace, seat of the Dalai Lama and spiritual centre of Tibetan Buddhism, rises on the hill in the background.
(Photo courtesy of the Royal Geographical Society.)

character traits or that there is a mountaineering 'type' can easily produce an absurd caricature. What is typical; a large bearded character with a far-away look in his eyes? This is pure farce. Bonington has remarked that all the adventurers he met when researching his book *Quest for Adventure* had a far-away look in their eyes *and large hands.* Perhaps they did. There have even been suggestions, on the basis of a few quite false examples, such as Bill Tilman, that mountaineers are all misogynists.

It is absurd to suggest that mountaineers conform to a physical type, that they are all anti-social, or even that they are any more egocentric than anyone else. But perhaps it is not altogether absurd to suggest that most of the best are not natural 'committee men', or good at taking orders they disagree with. Later in life Younghusband was a very active committee man, being President of the Royal Geographical Society and Chairman of the Mount Everest Committee, but he had the reputation of being fractious. And of course he was in charge. On the Tibetan expedition he was only a Colonel, but he behaved like a General. He was under the orders of administrators whom he regarded as incompetent. Worse, they had saddled him with a military escort whose commander was extremely cautious. One can't help remembering Doug Scott's analysis of large mountaineering expeditions. There is organised policy – the over-ground leadership – and the policy the leading climbers make up as they go along. Scott does not really believe in leadership – not anyone else's at any rate – and neither did Younghusband. When he got back to India and found the Secretary of State not as pleased with his efforts as he felt he should be, he refused to eat humble pie but weighed in with a spirited attack on the faults of bureaucracies and his political masters. This was not very diplomatic, but it did the mountaineer in him great credit.

Younghusband's fall from grace was nothing unusual. Interestingly, one of his staff on the Tibet mission was a young subaltern, F.M. Bailey, whose subsequent adventures as a political officer and spy of British interests are amongst the most remarkable of Central Asian political history, but he ended up crusty and disillusioned, believing himself unappreciated and passed over by inferior men. Bailey was to play a small but crucial part in Everest history, because as political officer in Sikkim in the 1920s he did his best to frustrate the early expeditions to the mountain. And there is no reason why this should surprise us. The fact that a man has been a great adventurer himself is in itself no reason to expect him to encourage others.

Younghusband was perhaps luckier, because after the Tibet episode he found a vocation which completely absorbed him for the remainder of his life. This was nothing less than the attempt to understand the spiritual dimension of the human condition, to recognise it in all the religions of mankind, however diverse, and to encourage the world to follow his example and work for universal love and understanding.

There is no doubt that Younghusband's experiences of Tibet and of Asia generally affected him deeply. Alone on a mountainside after signing his treaty with the Tibetans, he felt buoyed up on a wave of elation which would do very well as an example of one of Bourdillon's 'moments'; 'I felt in touch with the flaming heart of the world. What was glowing in all Creation and in every single human being was a joy as far beyond mere goodness as the light of the sun is beyond the glow of a candle. Never again could I think evil. Never again could I bear enmity . . .' Younghusband expressed such sentiments many times. On the return journey from Lhasa, and not yet aware of his superiors' wrath, he wrote: 'I was insensibly suffused with an almost intoxicating sense of elation and goodwill. This exhilaration of the moment grew and grew until it thrilled through me with overpowering intensity. . . . All nature and all humanity were bathed in a rosy glowing radiancy . . .'.

These experiences could have been recorded by any number of modern mountaineers – Joe Tasker for example. The rewards the mountains offer have not changed in the slightest. But with Younghusband the exhilaration is allowed to become something more, to become an intellectual position about the world rather than a purely emotional reaction, and to feed a growing belief that all peoples can understand each other and come together whilst maintaining the integrity of their own particular faiths. And Joe would never have fallen for that. In the World Council of Faiths which he founded in the 1930s, Younghusband aimed to bring together not just different Christian denominations but all religious systems. 'The man', wrote one of his obituarists, 'was greater than his message.' Perhaps; or the message was greater than men.

Younghusband wrote some thirty works of religious philosophy, and a discussion of them is beyond the scope of this book. But time and again he used not only mountains but mountaineering itself as a symbol of the spiritual quest, and the way he did so is both interesting and questionable.

His style we must put to one side. 'The struggle of man with the mountain continues apace. Man reels back again and again. But again and again he returns to the onslaught', he writes in the Foreword to Frank Smythe's *Kamet Conquered*. This is typical Younghusband prose. But he ends the same introduction: 'We may be certain also that, in pitting himself against the mountain, man will himself have added to his stature and be better able for loftier living'. This is a major claim, and it is what makes a consideration of Younghusband important.

What evidence is there that mountaineering makes man 'better able for loftier living'? The primitive life-style which Younghusband knew so well from his travels was for ever pitting itself against mountains, and he believed it had a value. Probably we would agree. But when Younghusband talked about pitting onself against the mountain he meant that mountaineering *as a pastime* added to man's stature and improved his spiritual possibilities. He did not mean native peoples living among the mountains, but Westerners coming from the other side of the world. This is why in his later years he was so vociferous and untiring in promoting attempts on Everest. From a position of influence in the committee rooms of the Royal Geographical Society, Younghusband wanted the mountain climbed, and he wrote confidently of the spiritual benefit to be derived from it. He had no doubts.

But the truth is that there was little time for spirituality at 28,000 ft in a Norfolk jacket and tweeds, and many early Everesters, not just Mallory, had little time for Tibet. The situation is no different today. High-altitude climbers are often egocentric and narrow-minded individuals who behave abominably to each other and care for nothing but getting to the top. The spiritual pilgrimage argument begins to look rather thin.

Mountaineering and the spiritual quest were connected in Younghusband's mind in two ways. In the first place mountaineering could be a symbol, the physical challenge a metaphor, of the spiritual challenge facing us. As his biographer put it, 'The principle of bodily acclimatisation to high altitudes was the symbol of a far diviner principle: the acclimatisation of the human spirit to the realm of the eternal'. There is little to argue with here, and it is interesting to note that throughout his involvement with Everest affairs Younghusband consistently supported a policy of slow physical acclimatisation as the key to climbing at altitude. He was not keen on the use of bottled oxygen, even when most of the mountaineering establishment supported it.

But secondly there was the actual experiencing of mountains and mountaineering, and here Younghusband's view that mountaineering is almost bound to be spiritually 'good' looks much more dubious. It gave rise to an equally shaky educational ideal. 'The contemplation of any great mountain has an elevating influence upon a man', he wrote. Well, sometimes. His conclusion? That efforts should be made to seek out the finest mountain views in the Himalaya and make them known to the general public.

Now, this is outdoor education with a vengeance, and outdoor education has never been an altogether happy business, because despite its high ideals and many fine achievements it also epitomises the aphorism that we destroy that which we most love. No-one has yet discovered how the mountains can be popularised without also being ruined; certainly Younghusband did not. No doubt if we all went to the mountains with an enlightened attitude we would not destroy them as much as we do; but if we were not ignorant and foolish there would probably be no need to go anyway. Lunn was surely right when he wrote that 'though the individual mountaineer is entitled to claim that he is a better man than he would have been if he had never climbed, he should not imply that he is a better man than those who detest all forms of active and dangerous sport. Samuel Johnson was no ascetic. He disliked mountains and detested solitude, and was seldom happy outside the congenial atmosphere of London, but he was a better man than most mountaineers'.

Everest: would climbing it degrade it in some way, destroy a symbol which was better left untouched? We often feel that way today about untouched areas of the world and such feelings have, I believe, a religious meaning. The religious temperament is appalled that in the modern world everything can be touched; *nothing is sacred any more*. People with a religious temperament, and thus a need for the sacred, often look to satisfy it in mountains, but it is becoming a more and more difficult search.

Younghusband's view was rather different. 'The mountain now stands there proud and erect and unconquered. And the faint-hearted peoples around it fear to approach it. They have the capacity of body to reach the summit any year they liked. But they are lacking in spirit. All they attain to is the painting of pictures depicting the fierce anger of gods repelling the English who dared to approach them. For all that the mountain is doomed. Man knows the worst about it. He knows exactly the way in which he can creep up it. He knows the extremes of frost and snow and tempest that defend it. But he knows also that the mountain remains stationary in capacity for defence while he is increasing in capacity to conquer.' Younghusband was perfectly happy that thousands of men and women had climbed Mont Blanc, and he saw no reason to feel differently about Everest. To Younghusband there simply wasn't a problem here. But I wonder if he would feel the same if he was alive today. You cannot totally humanise Christ and expect him to retain his power; so too, you cannot tramp all over every mountain in the world and expect them to retain their spiritual value.

In claiming 'it doesn't matter' Younghusband was envisaging summit climbers not as *prima donnas* but as representatives of all mankind merely fulfilling what had been prepared by their predecessors. But this was naive. It is not his personal experiences one would quarrel with, but what he read into them. The mystic vision which came to him through mountaineering was a 'living at lightning velocity' – a good phrase, as good as the 'intricacies of thought enough to fry the circuits of a computer' coined more recently by Greg Child. He was fascinated by scientists' and philosophers' speculations on the connection of diverse things, the all-pervasive influence of every object, 'cosmic consciousness'. Like the mystics, he saw not the differences in religious creeds but the similarities in religious experience of all races and times. But he read into the primitive mind innocence, and into mountaineering a potential for enlightenment and bringing native peoples and western visitors together, which now seems too optimistic.

'God', says Don Cupitt, 'is the sum of our values.' Today He is less and less an omnipotent Being and more and more a representation of the complete self. We recognise ourselves as inconsistent and contradictory, as composed of what Gurdjieff called 'the many conflicting I's', each of which has quite different values, beliefs and interests. We carry within ourselves both Heaven and Hell, God and the Devil. The conscious mind lives in passing time, with achievement and egocentricity; beneath is the 'shadow', the primal man, still there and still demanding satisfaction.

Spiritual evolution is then the gradual accomplishment of harmony, the religious goal the integrating of different aspects of the self into a whole. It is not an integration that is logically comprehensible, but one would not expect it to be. The religious life must soon go beyond what can be explained, or even understood. It must also go beyond 'the world'. The evolved man understands all, accepts all, and is yet detached from it.

Has this got anything at all to do with mountaineering? 'The aim of the mountaineer', Bernard Amy has written, 'is to take the place of the Zen Sage'. This may be true of mountaineering in the widest sense, it may be true of the ascetic wanderer, and it *can* be true of modern mountaineering. There is, for example, time to contemplate. Those endless weeks spent at Base Camp or sitting out storms – one of the attractions of expeditions is that they can be a very convenient excuse for doing nothing but sitting and thinking. The mountaineer is sometimes given that time which Blake insisted was the prime requisite of spiritual insight. And there are those 'moments' when the silence of the mountains presses in and combines with our own elation to produce a feeling of eternity in the present, and we understand a little better the words of William Law: 'man was put into this world for no other purpose than to arise out of the vanity of time'. That is a real religious experience, and so are all experiences of 'fusion in diversity'.

But the average climbing experience is less highfalutin' – not because it is selfish (a characteristic of many divines), but because it is narrow. That is precisely why traditional mountaineering fears fanaticism; it narrows the game, and so destroys any possibility of spiritual seriousness. Generally speaking, it would be ludicrous to equate the modern mountaineer with the Zen Sage. All mountaineering can do is remind one that one *could* be a Zen Sage, and perhaps should be, if one was not being a climber. It produces a glimpse of spiritual possibilities. Doug Scott puts it well. After his successful ascent of Everest with Dougal Haston in 1975:

> I came down with ambition fulfilled, and an empty space for noble thoughts and feelings; but I knew that space would soon be swamped back in the city – it had happened before. ...'

And that is the only religious value that mountaineering can confidently claim. Life opens up a little, and one sees the possibility not just of achievement but of a wider form of human evolution. But for that evolution to take place? That is a very different thing.

Doug Scott, now in his early 50s and one of the world's leading Himalayan mountaineers, is well known to have deep philosophical interests. These have yet to be distilled definitively, and an autobiography from Scott remains one of the more obvious gaps in the literature. His thesis seems to be that 'normality' eats away at our intuitive faculties and awareness of life, both of which need not only space but our experiences on the edge of things – danger, suffering, simplicity – if they are to survive, and that without them we are divorced from all that is most profound and satisfying in life – to say nothing of morality.

By focusing on intuition and the importance of hard-won experience in developing it, Scott has inherited Whillans' mantle in some ways – though Whillans, on the surface at least, showed none of Scott's anguish.
(Photo: Paul Braithwaite, early 1980s.)

The Ganesh Himal of Nepal, seen above valley mist from Laurebina, Gosainkund, in the crisp, clear air of November. This shot typifies the wonderful mountain scenery which is drawing trekkers to the Himalaya in ever-increasing numbers.
(Photo: Richard Gibbens, 1989.)

7 Conditioning in Time

What makes a piece of scenery beautiful to a mountaineer? It would be convenient if it could be defined explicitly, as one might define the picturesque. Certain proportions; certain colours perhaps; certain elements of design balancing and improving each other. Mountain-lovers might then be clearer than they are as to what it is they wish to preserve.

Such analyses have been attempted on many occasions. The Victorian explorers of the European Alps in particular felt they had discovered not just a new field of action but a new field of aesthetic appreciation, and, understandably, they wanted to make sense of it. They defined the 'best' Alpine view not as the close-up or the distant panorama, but the middle distance; in a connected way, they believed the most satisfying views were to be obtained not from the tops of the highest mountains or from the valleys but from somewhere in between: '. . . for the thorough enjoyment of an Alpine view there is nothing like a mountain of from ten to twelve thousand feet, provided it is sufficiently distant from overtopping peaks.'

But unfortunately, what people found beautiful in practice had an awkward habit of ignoring these hard-won rules. Beauty proved to be inconsistent and unpredictable, and one must say that in the end Victorian Alpinists were no more successful than anyone else in laying down simple explicit criteria. Nor were the early Himalayan pioneers. When mountaineers finally got themselves to the north side of Everest in the 1920s some thought it a vision of supreme beauty; others agreed with George Finch: 'a ponderous, ungainly, ill-proportioned lump'.

And though in answer to the question: are not the British hills as beautiful in their way as anywhere else? most people would surely have no hesitation in answering 'yes', there are those who disagree. Longstaff, for example, wrote that 'For beauty of sculptured form and variety of setting they cannot compare with the Alps, the Caucasus, or the Himalaya. But they are mountains and they have their own intrinsic quality'. This is one of Longstaff's more lame remarks, and a clear lesson that the itch to do the impossible – define the objective criteria of mountain beauty – will lead the best of us to ramble if given the chance. Such discussions rarely get anywhere, and it is a mistake to get involved with them.

The problem is not simply one of semantics (what one man calls terrifying another might call beautiful, meaning exactly the same thing). It is that what we find beautiful and what ugly is highly sensitive to cultural assumptions. In mathematics, say, one gets away from that. Mathematics is beautiful; everyone who understands mathematics agrees, and there has been no change here since the days of Euclid and Pythagoras. Mathematics has a harmony and a delight for those who understand it irrespective of the age they live in. And if this attitude can be extended to certain aspects of the visual arts, it is only to those which operate more or less independently of the natural world. When 'the world' is involved, things invariably become difficult. One cannot, for example, imagine the beauty of landscape art ever being defined independently of cultural conditioning. If that were possible we would be able to say which was better: English eighteenth century Landscape or French Impressionism. Nor can one see it happening in our reaction to natural art, and in our feelings towards mountain scenery least of all.

In mountaineering, beauty is not to do with formal criteria so much as with psychological affectiveness. Thus beauty may make us shudder, it may bring a feeling of pure pleasure, it may be picturesque and calming. Almost anything can be beautiful; *the only important thing is that it should wake us up.* And what succeeds in doing that depends at least in part of what we have been taught to love or on what has associations for us. Much of the beauty of the British hills clearly arises from association, and it is therefore a lost cause for Longstaff or anyone else to try to fit them into a 'pecking order' with other mountains. The Victorian pioneers thought the Alps beautiful. Well, that is hardly surprising; they were new, and they had happy associations. In the second half of the nineteenth century the Victorians had a field day in what was virtually an untouched playground, and it would be extraordinary if they did not think well of it and feel prejudiced in its favour. It is perfectly understandable that they should then concoct spurious reasons for thinking Mont Blanc more beautiful than, say, Mt Everest; just as it is equally understandable if we now feel differently.

It is a commonplace to say that the modern enthusiasm for mountains springs from our situation. The West long regarded high hills as an abomination; now we think them admirable. Gray, on a tour of the Alps, felt not only that there was 'not a precipice, not a torrent, not a cliff, but is pregnant with religion and poetry', but also that 'there are certain scenes that would awe an atheist into belief'. Belief in quite what was open to doubt, but here at least was the realisation that we had been missing something. So whilst Thomas Burnet could write of the Alps: 'They have neither Form nor Beauty, nor Shape, nor Order, no more than the Clouds of the Air. Then how barren, how desolate . . .', he also felt that 'There is something august and stately in the Air of these things that inspires the mind with great thoughts and passions . . .' Joseph Addison, who visited Switzerland in 1701, defined the feeling more exactly: 'you have a near prospect of the Alps, which are broken into so many steps and precipices, that *they fill the mind with an agreeable kind of horror*' (my italics). 'Agreeable horror' is precisely the feeling that Gray was to express about Lodore Falls in the English Lake District a century later and that modernist writers are still expressing today. Medieval thought looked on mountains with disfavour, thinking them a distraction from the contemplation of God. By Addison's time, the world was taking a different view.

Such changing attitudes say very little about human nature but a great deal about people's circumstances. As a result of its successful exploitation of the natural world the western world had, by the eighteenth century, come to feel confident and secure in the face of nature and wilderness, so attitudes towards such places changed and instead of seeing in them all sorts of exaggerated dangers, such as dragons and demons – dangers which were no more than an allegory of a state of mind, in fact a form of animism – people at last saw mountains for what they are.

Or did they? What they are is inanimate stone, and the romantic view, which is still with us, can be accused of being as over-enthusiastic as the medieval view had been unsympathetic. Where there had once been demons and dragons there was now man's 'true' home, the place he was meant to be. Mountains and wild country in general became idealised.

If attitudes to mountains depend on time and place, the same is true of the style in which mountaineering is practised. Mummery dispensed with guides because improved information and increasing numbers were rendering the old ways too tame. Today many rock-climbers undertake physical training – they did not in Mummery's time – because that is now the only way to raise standards. These are changes in style, but they do not imply changes in underlying motivation.

Geography affects style. The Himalayas would seem to be infinitely superior to the Alps but for most mountaineers the Alps are nearer, so from the late eighteenth century to the present day they have played an inordinately large part in mountaineering history. The British hills provide an even more extreme example. Looked at as 'facts', as inanimate stone, British crags and hills are inescapably minor, yet their importance to mountaineering development has been enormous. Why? Convenience certainly. But perhaps they have also permeated some sort of collective consciousness because we live with them and through them so continuously. It may be that even if the Himalayas were to become as cheap and easy, these places would still maintain their interest for us.

Mountain ranges are natural geographic boundaries and in many cases have come to form political boundaries too. And political boundaries shape style. Thus in the early days of the West's exploration of the Himalaya the British enjoyed invaluable advantages of status and freedom, and the British Empire, more specifically a British passport, was the key to a great many places otherwise inaccessible. Everest is the obvious example. The British had access to Everest, off and on, decades before anyone else did. No other country made an attempt to climb the mountain before the Swiss in 1952; the British made some eight attempts before succeeding on their ninth in '53. This was purely political luck for the British, and bad luck on everyone else.

The history of mountaineering is largely the history of the privileged. Since mountain-climbing requires money, or, if not money, time, it was for many years dominated by the middle-aged upper classes. There was little opportunity for brash young superstars to climb in the greater ranges, or indeed in the Alps. So when the British attacked Everest in the 1920s they carried both a good deal of well-connected dead weight and too much age. As part of the era's style this was understandable enough, but it encouraged the erroneous

With the north side of Everest in the background (that 'ponderous, ungainly, ill-proportioned lump'), members of the 1936 British Everest Expedition enjoy lunch *al fresco.*
(Photo courtesy of the Royal Geographical Society.)

belief, which lasted an astonishingly long time, that only the middle-aged performed well in the Himalaya; the young were thought to lack stamina. It is now clear that what they actually lacked was opportunity.

When people first began to go to the hills in large numbers this did not prove the emergence of a new sort of human being; it represented the rise of leisure. That much of the early exploration was done by the intellectual classes is not evidence that the mountains are too ethereal or spiritual to be appreciated by the working classes; it is a reminder that intellectuals often had long university holidays. In Britain in the 1920s and '30s it was often the unemployed working classes, not the intellectuals, who made the running; not because they were working class but because they were unemployed. In modern societies, there is a leisure class at both ends of the income spectrum, and mountaineering demands leisure in large quantities.

Even the spirit of a nation and a time plays its part. Nazi fervour does not explain German successes in the Alps in the '30s, but a sense of national resurgence was certainly a factor. And national pride played a large part in British successes in the nineteenth century, when Victorian climbers partook of that general confidence which came from being rulers of a great Empire at the height of its power and influence. It gave them a belief in themselves and in the rightness of what they were doing which now seems like a period piece, but was crucial at the time. As Ronald Clark put it, the Victorian pioneers felt that 'nature would be disregarding its proper laws if it held off too long the attacks of a properly led British party'. They took that sentiment with them when they began to explore further afield, and it combined admirably with political advantage to produce the unique style of the eccentric British explorer.

The availability of equipment affects style too. The clothing that the early Everest climbers used would today be regarded as quite inadequate, and although it did not stop them getting to within a thousand feet of the summit, modern clothing has undoubtedly extended mountaineers' performances. So have various technical inventions. At the end of the nineteenth century when alpinists turned their attention to new routes on mountains that had already been climbed, it was rock-climbs that resulted, not ice-climbs. This was not because the early climbers were not interested in ice but because the necessary equipment was not yet in existence. Rudimentary crampons seem to go back to the dawn of history and it must always have been obvious to anyone with a little ingenuity that some sort of spikes on the bottom of boots would make them grip better on snow; but crampons with front points that can be used on steep ice are a twentieth century development. And they made new things possible. The first ascent of the North Face of the Eiger in 1938 owed much to improved crampon design. Until recently, the invention of various devices for the protection of rock-climbs has had much the same effect, in that it has revolutionised style without changing the fundamental motives or rewards. The changes here, however, are now such that some modern rock-climbing, specifically 'sport' climbing, has precious little to do with traditional mountaineering and has more in common with Olympic gymnastics.

Leslie Stephen preferred the Alps to the Himalaya, but he was too wise a man to try to justify his preference on formal grounds. Instead, he admitted candidly that it was conditioned by his era and his personal experience. 'Savagery, pure and simple, the deathly solitude of the moon, even the Karakoram, would, I fear, make me shiver', he wrote. That was a very reasonable sentiment in the nineteenth century, when the Himalaya must indeed have seemed too awesome and unknown for comfort. Just as it is now equally reasonable for us to feel differently.

Nevertheless, one cannot help wondering whether the Victorians had not hit on something rather more fundamental in their enthusiasm for the Alps. Many argued that it arose from their being able to look down on villages and cultivation in the valleys from the summits. That made one feel more secure, and the scene became more attractive as a result. And this ability to see into the valleys also helped one to grasp the scale of the place. The Himalaya are so vast, and there is often no sign of human activity or anything else to which to anchor a sense of scale. The Alps are smaller, but what they have is more effectively used, perhaps so effectively that it can never be bettered.

The idea that the Alps represent some sort of optimum was put forward quite explicitly by several of the Victorian pioneers. The Scotsman James Forbes, the first Briton to climb a virgin Alpine peak,* suggested in his *Travels through the Alps* in 1843 that it is this ability to grasp the scale of the European mountains which is the key to our love of them. 'Their scale is sufficiently great to afford to at least nine-tenths of travellers the most majestic conceptions with which such objects can at all inspire them.' Not only do the signs of man offer a contrast and thus a context to the peaks, but there is an optimum point for the affectiveness of grandeur and scale on our sensibilities anyway. There is no point in searching for larger and larger objects *ad infinitum*; beyond a certain point one is simply unable to grasp anything more. And the parallel with the problem of extreme experience in general is inescapable. Terror, pain, suffering; it has a purpose – up to a point. But the utterly terrified or agonised man is reduced to a gibbering wreck, and the extreme ascetic to a pervert.

Affectiveness of scale is presumably independent of historical eras, cultural conditioning or associations, and dependent only on the capabilities of the human mind. So if Forbes' point was valid in 1843 it is still valid today, which means that for the sightseer, whose experience is purely visual, the Himalaya may be no more powerful than the Alps. If one is undertaking physical action, climbing or trekking, that is a different matter, but can anyone appreciate the superior scale of the Asian ranges purely by sightseeing from a hotel balcony? Not only are the major precipices of the Alps comparable to most things in the Himalaya, (the bases of Himalayan mountains start so much higher), but it is doubtful whether any increase in vertical interval above ten or twelve thousand feet means much to

---

*This was the Stockhorn (11,796ft) in the *Valais*, Swiss Alps, close to the Matterhorn. There are several Stockhorns in the Alps; since Forbes's ascent this one has been renamed the Wandfluhhorn.

Mountaineering expeditions involve so much more than climbing: here, porters are negotiating the Hispar Gorge during the walk-in to Kunyang Kish, central Karakoram, in 1980. On terrain like this, as well as on the mountain, crampons and ropes are ethically allowable, and can be useful. To by-pass it with a helicopter, however, would be to alter the whole nature of the game.
(Photo: the author.)

the visual senses anyway. Perhaps the best way to decide this question would be by visiting not the Himalaya but Mt McKinley in Alaska, whose relatively modest summit of 20,000ft nevertheless rises from snowfields at a mere 3000ft, thus producing a mountain face as large as any in the world.

There is certainly *some* point at which increased size ceases to make any difference. The size of the universe might be anything so far as our ability to be awed by it is concerned. A million light years or a million million, it is all the same. Rock-climbers have often remarked that yawning abysses of a few hundred feet can be as frightening, or more frightening, than those of a few thousand.

The visual impression produced by a mountain is thus a psychological and subjective matter rather than a purely objective one. Such an approach was well established in aesthetic theory by the middle of the eighteenth century. 'Every Thing that is *new* or *uncommon* raises a Pleasure in the Imagination, because it fills the Soul with an agreeable Surprise, gratifies its Curiosity, and gives it an Idea of which it was not before possest . . . It is this that bestows Charms on a Monster, and makes even the Imperfections of Nature please us', wrote Addison. In other words it wakes us up. This is what was meant by the sublime; that which, as George Santayana put it, makes 'the mind recoil upon itself'. It was the grand or the usual, working its effect on us through impressiveness of scale or, if that was not enough, through fright. It was above all something intense, to be found through towering precipices and torrents, or anything else which sent a thrill of fear and wonder down one's spine. It was not for cultured discussions in country drawing rooms, but to be experienced. The crux was to feel, and man needs contrast in order to feel. The sublime might not be enjoyable at all in the sense that fields of waving corn or an idyll of Arcadia are enjoyable. It is difficult to feel aesthetic pleasure whilst cold, tired or frightened, as any mountaineer can confirm. But one certainly feels alive, and a more conventional enjoyment can come later.

Because its basis was psychological the sublime was irrational, even cruel. Pain, Edmund Burke was to claim, is a stronger emotion than pleasure. Indeed: 'I am convinced that we have a degree of delight, and that no small one, in the real misfortunes and pains of others . . . for terror is a passion which always produces delight when it does not press too close . . .' This goes far beyond aesthetics. One remembers Boardman and Tasker descending from Changabang to find the tragedy of the American expedition. 'This was the sensation of life, the sense that we remained . . .'

It is hardly surprising that several key figures of the Romantic Movement, Blake for example, were hostile to Burke's theories of the sublime. Blake was a high Romantic, a believer in deliverance through the human imagination rather than mere sensations. Mountaineers on the other hand are in their element with Burke.

The part that should be played by the human imagination is at the core of the disagreement between a high Romantic aesthetician such as Blake or Ruskin and a highly civilised but nevertheless dedicated mountaineer like Leslie Stephen. For Ruskin, a high

John Ruskin (1819–1900) in the early 1880s.

In the fourth volume of *Modern Painters* (1850) Ruskin wrote: 'To myself, mountains are the beginning and the end of all natural scenery; in them, and in the forms of inferior landscape that lead to them, my affections are wholly bound up; and though I can look with happy admiration at the lowland flowers, and woods, and open skies, the happiness is tranquil and cold, like that of examining detached flowers in a conservatory, or reading a book. . . . But the slightest rise and fall in the road – a mossy bank at the side of a crag of chalk, with brambles at its brow, overhanging it – a ripple over three or four stones in the stream by the bridge – above all, a wild bit of ferny ground under a fir or two, looking as if, possibly, one might see a hill if one got to the other side of the trees, will instantly give me intense delight, because the shadow, or the hope, of the hills is in them.'

Ruskin may not have approved of climbing, but anyone who feels like this is essentially 'one of us.'
(Photo courtesy of Abbot Hall Art Gallery and Museum, Kendal.)

valuation of the imagination is virtually an article of faith. One should be able to imagine these strong sensations and remember what the mountains mean without giving in to 'greased pole' technique. To Ruskin, the mountaineer is a sort of heretic because he has thrown over imagination and descended to mere physique. Ruskin's position is linked with a stronger feeling for the sacred too. For him mountaineers are not only heretics but despoilers. Mountains, as sacred objects, should not be trampled.

To Stephen, on the other hand, it is precisely the hands-on approach which enables one to really appreciate what the mountains are and what they mean. It is no good Ruskin wishing we all had superlative imaginative faculties; the fact is, we do not – as the inability of the human senses to appreciate the Himalaya over and above the Alps makes only too clear. Even the most vital aesthete may be impotent here. That being so, the best thing is to experience at first hand, to gain 'what theologians would call an experimental faith in the size of mountains – to substitute a real living belief for a dead intellectual assent'. There are, after all, things that can never be imagined. Imagination has its powers but mountaineering, actually doing it, has more.

It comes down to a question of means, for the ends sought by Ruskin and Stephen were not so different. In *Modern Painters* Ruskin discussed looking at the Alps and trying to conjure up their associations. He found that one's emotions handed on 'a curious web of subtle fancy and imperfect knowledge'. One's ideas of the mountains' size were 'vague', one's grasp of eternity and one's own relative transitoriness 'pathetic'. Yet '. . . so long as we see that the *feeling* is true, we pardon, or are even pleased by, the confessed fallacy of sight which it induces . . .'

It was the same aim: elation, through an expanding world and the deep comfort of the unchanging inextricably combined. The mountain scene should suggest new things and new horizons, but it should also suggest the eternal and unchangeable with all that implies about human littleness, nature's magnificence, and a union between the two. A scene can strike us as beautiful because it suggests new worlds or because it suggests acceptance, but ideally it should convey both.

When this fusion is captured on paper the result is art. The landscape painting of ancient China, depicting the meditative wandering scholar crossing a footbridge below sublime crags and surrounded by nature, achieved it many centuries ago. Photography too is capable of suggesting not the finite or the infinite, not ourselves or the universe, but both. Walking is rhythmic, and it soothes because it re-establishes contact with the way things are. The mountain scene, affecting us purely visually, can be soothing for precisely the same reason, whether the rhythm is of undulating hills retreating to a dusty haze at infinity or of seasonal change, spring mornings and autumn colours. Most mountain photography attempts nothing more and is pretty, commercially successful, and unobjectionable. But beyond it lies the photography which delights the mountaineer; pictures which seem to lead you on, so that you long to be there yourself, whilst still maintaining a sense of wilderness and space. And beyond that again are images which suggest not merely

The author and companion above Kishtwar, Indian Himalaya, after crossing the watershed from Zanskar in 1978.
(Photo: Hamish Fulton.)

new physical horizons of undiscovered country, but new horizons of the human mind and the borders of the visionary.

Some years ago I met the art photographer Hamish Fulton in the Arctic and afterwards we went to India together, walking over the Himalayan watershed from the dry plains of Zanskar to the lush valleys of Kishtwar. Hamish had no interest in the technical sophistication of modern photography. He ambled along with minimal equipment and claimed to know nothing about the making of the large black and white prints from which he earns his living. He just recorded what he saw. But like a painter, like any true artist, he changed the way I saw it.

Mountain beauty, like mountaineering, is composed of contradictions, and that makes it vulnerable. The first page of *Mr West's Guide to the Lakes in Cumberland, Westmorland and Lancashire*, an influential popularisation of the new fashion for mountain scenery which appeared at the turn of the eighteenth century, tries to reassure us that 'the local knowledge here communicated will not, however, injure, much less prevent, the agreeable surprise that attends the first sight of scenes that surpass all description, and of objects which will always affect the spectator in the highest degree'. Not so! With that and a thousand statements like it mountain-lovers admitted their awareness of an aesthetic problem which exactly mirrors that facing physical action.

Reverting to aesthetic terminology, one might say that mountain beauty is made up of an uneasy combination of sensations and associations. The drawback of relying on sensations is clear – the lure of the extreme, which leads one ever onwards. But associations, even pleasant ones, have drawbacks too. Aestheticians tell us that associations are one of the secrets of beauty, and mountaineers would agree, but the situation is not easy. Sir Martin Conway was alarmed when he looked across the Rhone Valley to the Pennine Alps during his epic walk though the Alps in 1892; alarmed not by his reaction but by the lack of it:

> The view, I suppose, is wonderful, but it did not move me, and I asked myself why. The answer seems to be that I was too familiar with every detail in it. There was scarcely a peak in sight, great or small, that I had not climbed, not a valley that I had not penetrated. Every object was swathed in reminiscences. There may be a charm in this kind of retrospect, but it is not the charm of beauty.

In mountaineering, charm is not enough. It is far too mediocre a feeling. There is mountain beauty which impresses and mountain beauty which soothes, but the one quality which is indispensable is the intensity to wake us up. And too many associations, like too much knowledge, kills that.

Sensations and associations are both necessary; it is only their relative importance which alters with age and experience and so leads to a change in our feeling for mountains. The young climber is exhilarated by the savage, the close-up and the far panorama, and much less by the aesthetics of the middle distance and the balanced harmonious view. The attraction of the balanced view may have an involuntary basis in all of us, but there is still a sense in which one must learn to love it and the only teacher is experience. In time, doubts about the purely terrifying creep in. How far can it go? Like the extreme experience, which cannot go on for ever except to disaster, the extreme scene loses all meaning and becomes merely indulgent.

But to appreciate that one must first experience it. Then, but for most of us only then, can one proceed to put a greater emphasis on imagination. Only after experience does the extreme cease to dominate and find its place as a part of a greater whole. Only then are we in a position to agree with Schiller: beauty 'cannot on the one hand be purely physical, as the degrading taste of our day would have it, and as has been held by shrewd observers (like Burke) who relied too much on empirical evidence; nor, on the other hand, can it be pure form, as has been thought by speculative philosophers, who left experience too far behind . . .' What it becomes is 'the interplay of two opposed impulses and the union of two opposed principles', or as Coleridge put it (and Coleridge understood the attractions of the extreme only too well) '. . . that in which the many, still seen as many, becomes one'.

But a change in visual taste is only part of a more general change which almost every climber undergoes with age and experience, and which amounts to a rebalancing of the finite and infinite in life. When one is young it is as Winthrop Young said: mountaineering is a celebration of vitality and strength, with 'the song of life humming through the silence'. The young say extreme action is necessary. Why? To awaken one's senses. But it is a law of diminishing returns, both aesthetically and physically. 'Have you ever really wanted something and after a lot of effort you finally get it?' asked Tomo Cesen after soloing the south face of the world's fourth highest mountain, Lhotse. 'Well, that's roughly how I felt. I know though, that Lhotse took part of my soul. The part that every so often wants to feel uncertainty and true adventure where decisions have to [be] made and acted on continuously.' On the summit of an eight thousander, far from thinking or feeling anything extraordinary, one is unlikely to think or feel much at all. 'No feeling of sublimity. I am too tired for that', wrote Messner of Everest. 'I should be thinking great thoughts', thought Boardman on Kanchenjunga, 'but none came'.

There is only a 'solution' to this in the sense that there are different solutions appropriate to different stages in one's life. Experienced mountaineers, as Haston said, are those who have been in a number of risky situations and been lucky enough to survive them. And survival can lead to change. Eric Shipton, for example, was changed by experiencing two particularly large and terrifying avalanches on Everest in the 1930s. It is usual to be thrusting when young and more accepting when older, and most climbers have their closest shaves in youth and later in life try harder to avoid them. It is ignorant to say that one shouldn't risk one's neck, because we know quite well that doing so has a unique pay-off. Was Mummery wrong on Nanga Parbat? No; but that does not stop us being sorry that he did not live through it, and so experience another and equally valuable form of illumination. The same can be said of most climbers who have done impressive, risky things and come to a bad end. What is distressing is not the end but its being untimely. *What is distressing is that the spiritual adventure is left incomplete.*

Extreme climbing is dangerous, time-consuming and expensive. Age brings other things to spend the money on, less free time, and responsibilities to others which makes killing yourself a very selfish thing to do. Most mountaineers, even the best, come in time to downgrade their ambitions and their commitment and to enjoy the mountains in a less extreme form.

But there are also internal reasons, developments within one's experience of mountaineering itself, which can make one want to change. Other things being equal, experience strengthens imagination, and, as I have tried to argue in the course of this book, a healthy imagination undermines physical action. One remembers the past and so imagines the future. So why go there? History itself becomes a form of experience, which by confusing one's sense of time brings its own joy. Is my friend Stephen Venables, Everest climber and so suddenly famous, the same gangling, bespectacled Stephen who seemed so much on the fringes when I first knew him? Running through the Rock and Ice era in the '50s, putting his own line into history, I know there is a wild Glaswegian character called Pat Walsh, whose short-sightedness led to his putting up hard routes by getting lost. Recently, I rented a cottage on the Isle of Skye from a man called Patsy Walsh who was sweet as pie, wore glasses like bottles, and sounded as if he had lived there all his life, gazing across the Sound of Sleat to the hills of Knoydart. In the glory of a West Highland heat-wave he mowed the rough lawn in front of the croft and planted potatoes in rows. This one too was as hard as nails. Was he the same man?

Galen Rowell has coined a good phrase for the core feeling that has to be there if one is to continue, and he felt it whilst tracking the Leopard on the Baltoro: optimistic expectation. 'At the heart of the climbing experience is a constant state of optimistic expectation', he writes, 'and when that state is absent there is no reason to continue climbing.' Life is for living and we admire people who do live it, and envy those who continue much as they always have because they still find in their climbing the same excitement and magic all of us had in the beginning. But for most of us, time and experience eat away at our 'optimistic expectation'.

I am reminded of two expeditions I took part in, attempting the second ascent of Kunyang Kish, a formidable peak of just under 26,000ft in the central Karakoram. In 1980 Dave Wilkinson, Stephen Venables and I laid siege to the virgin north ridge of the mountain in the most exciting and dangerous seven weeks of my life. None of us really knew what we were doing, none of us had climbed on such a high mountain before, and we moved unroped on the huge glacier slopes, exhilarated by our boldness and effectiveness. We took great risks, falling in crevasses and being lucky on more than one occasion not to go over the huge cornices of the ridge when they broke away just in front of us. Time and again we would wake in camp after heavy snowfalls to see the remains of windslab avalanches all around. Twice we descended the whole route wading though chest-deep snow, just waiting for the slopes to go but somehow being lucky. Everything was new, the

'That, if anything, was a time of optimistic expectation. . . .' The author on the glacier below the north-west spur of Kunyang Kish in 1980, with the north ridge behind, leading up to the summit at just under 25,800ft. *(Photo: Stephen Venables.)*

'Twice we descended the whole route wading through chest-deep snow, just waiting for the slopes to go but somehow being lucky.' Descending Kunyang Kish after heavy storms, August 1980.
(Photo: author's collecton.)

mountain was superb, and it really looked as if we were going to get up it. From our last camp we looked out along the final corniced ridge . . . so close. That, if anything, was a time of optimistic expectation. So we came back the following year to try and finish the job.

And for me that was very different. We were less innocent now. We knew how dangerous the route was, and most of it was known territory. And I had imagined that final ridge. Whether I really did or not, I *thought* I knew what the experience would be like, stepping out on the summit, the glory, the glow . . . And the optimistic expectation which had made our first attempt so rewarding was gone.

Perhaps that is what happened to the late Georges Bettembourg, who failed to get up the North Ridge of Kangchenjunga with Boardman, Tasker and Scott in 1979. Perhaps he persuaded himself he knew what it would be like:

> Peter and I waited for the day to break, hoping for the weather to improve. We dug a little platform for our feet, anchored our axes, and started hitting our feet and hands to keep them alive. 'Peter, we can say we've climbed this mountain! We're so close to the summit. I feel I've already been on top and climbed it . . .'
>
> "We're not yet on the summit!" Peter yelled into my face, cutting me short. Suddenly I realised that Peter and I were miles apart.

Optimistic expectation can be destroyed by experience, by too much information, or by too many people, and it is then time to turn to Tom Patey's ploys and climb down as gracefully as one can – or to find philosophical justifications for not climbing.*
But it would be a mistake to be too cynical about this, for philosophising is not always specious, and out of experience may grow a genuine belief that one's enthusiasm is simply too narrow. This sentiment comes over strongly in the writings of Jim Perrin, one of the most notable mountaineering essayists of the last 20 years. In *A Valediction*, an article written in the early '70s, Perrin announced he was giving up hard climbing, though one suspects he has often been about to give up and either not managed it or, like the addicted smoker, gone back to the habit in the end. So why does he write such articles? To try to persuade himself perhaps, to make it easier to follow his own advice

It is a key problem. Perrin is not simply trying to climb down, but is struggling with a religious temperament, the temperament which says one ought to develop. 'Take away my life oh Lord, for I am not better than my fathers' spoke the prophet Elijah. Taken literally it may seen extreme, but the sense is clear enough: the meaning of life lies in the attempt – not necessarily the success but at least the attempt – to develop spiritually rather than remain static. But unfortunately it's not as simple as that, for there is also Isaiah; 'Let us eat and drink for tomorrow we shall die'. From this point of view the heretics are not the people who refuse to change but all those who make insufficient efforts to appreciate life whilst they have it. Life, after all, is short, and happiness should be a more positive thing

---

*See *The Art of Climbing Down Gracefully*, *Mountain 16* (1971), and *One Man's Mountains*.

Jim Perrin, much maligned but passionately involved climber and writer, who is now in his mid-forties, forever giving up climbing but still loving it.
(Photo: John Beatty.)

than can be found simply in freedom from difficulties. Anyone who takes that on board and lives life intensely is spiritually serious, even if it means carrying on with risky undertakings until luck runs out. 'Passive happiness is slack and insipid, and soon grows mawkish and intolerable', warned William James. 'Some austerity and wintry negativity, some roughness, danger, stringency and effort, some no! no! must be mixed in . . .'

There is a memorable interview in which Perrin, in his role as mountaineering journalist, interviews Bonington at his home in the Lake District on the occasion of the latter's fiftieth birthday. Perrin is going through one of his recurring climbing-is-pointless phases but Bonington, full of enthusiasm, drags him out for an evening's bouldering and maintains a manic commentary on the fun of it all:

> "This first bit's tricky, you sort of . . . lunge . . . there . . . that's got it. Most I've ever done is three times across and back . . . terrific for getting you fit . . . this last section's *bloody* strenuous."

Perrin just gives up and watches, half envious at the way the man has maintained his enthusiasm for so long, half despising him for not being able to see beyond it. Is he a genius or an imbecile?

But if one should go beyond, then to what? To something wider, to something which faces up to the fact that one cannot go on climbing for ever and that no mature individual should want to. One suspects that Perrin is in reluctant agreement with Tom Price: 'Some people have it [the spirit of adventure] in greater measure than others. Some appear not to have it at all, and that, perhaps, is the mark of complete maturity'. One should try to grow out of this childish egocentricity; out of the absurd pretence, which hard climbing represents, that one is omnipotent. 'The ego and the will are the driving forces in climbing, the philosophy behind it is one of despair.'

And that is why that image of Younghusband's of climbing Everest as a sort of spiritual ascent is ultimately so absurd. It has a truth; when we climb the big mountains we disengage from the trivialities of life, rise above them both literally and metaphorically, and are given the opportunities of a wider perspective. We suffer, and we experience the ascetic life. One way or another we are forced to 'awake', and all of this constitutes a spiritual improvement. And yet . . . and yet no-one is more blind than the high altitude climber. In *The Odyssey* Sisyphus was compelled to roll a great stone up a hill, but as it reached the top the stone always rolled down, and Sisyphus had to begin all over again. For Reinhold Messner, the most celebrated mountaineer of our time, a climber is like Sisyphus, and 'the stone which I push up the mountain is my own psyche'. On the summit of Everest his feeling is not of an ending, of final enlightenment, but rather that 'I too shall have to roll that mythical stone all my life without ever reaching the summit'. . . .

Even in mountain symbolism it is an error to see only the snow-capped summit. One should pay equal attention to the massive base and rolling hills on which it rests. Evolution involves more than reaching summits.

Perrin recognised the hopelessness of going to ever greater extremes when he soloed

Coronation Street, one of the many fine British rock climbs put up by Bonington. It was a very bold thing to do, but it changed nothing. It merely brought a temporary feeling of elation – and then fright at the thought that he would probably do something similar again. Achieving is good; to feel your own individuality is good. But to go on and on like this is to move further and further from reality. It becomes truly neurotic, not closer but more distant from real enlightenment. 'The climbers', says Perrin, 'are lost not in God but in themselves.'

No-one's attitude can stand totally still. There is always some shift in emphasis from action to imagination. And always, something of the past is carried with you. 'If you detach yourself and observe it, so much is added to the enjoyment of a day out', observes Perrin, expressing a classic piece of Gurdjieffian psychology. But I doubt if he would have written like that when he first started climbing. 'There can be no classical mountain day without a conscious search for beauty', wrote Jerry Wright. But to make a conscious search you need the experience. And what is a classic mountain day? It is an experience in which, as in the classic climb, opposites, action and imagination, come to some sort of truce. The classic mountain day is something that the old guard are always promoting; it is also something which by definition only they can enjoy.

You have to experience the extreme and be lucky enough to survive it. '. . . The mountains had been a natural field of activity where, playing on the frontiers of life and death, we had found the freedom for which we were blindly groping', wrote Herzog. That is an explanation of why people climb with which we are by now completely familiar. But the extreme experience of climbing Annapurna and barely surviving changed him.

> . . . I was saved and I had won my freedom. This freedom, which I shall never lose . . . has given me the rare joy of loving that which I used to despise. A new and splendid life has opened out before me.

Herzog's frostbite injuries destroyed his climbing career; they also gave him an awareness of life which he would not otherwise have had. The man who can love that which he used to despise sounds like a superior man, and Herzog was able to turn his energies to other things.

> There are other Annapurnas in the lives of men.

It is a philosophy which his companion Louis Lachenal never achieved. A meteoric and brilliant climber and master of graceful movement, Lachenal too was dreadfully frostbitten, and would never again enjoy the glory of sheer physical mastery. But instead of changing he took up extreme skiing, and was killed in an avalanche four years after the Annapurna ascent.

The point is this: having experienced the extreme, do you change or not? Do you allow imagination in, or refuse to countenance it? Do you allow the extreme to continue to

'This freedom, which I shall never lose, . . .' Maurice Herzog (centre) and Louis Lachenal on stretchers after the first ascent of Annapurna in 1950. Prompt amputation by the expedition doctor saved both their lives, and Herzog, now in his 70s, went on to a distinguished political career. *(Photo: Herzog collection.)*

deliver its unique exhilaration, or fight it?

One of the best modern accounts of extreme action comes from rock-climbing: *The Only Blasphemy*, by the American John Long. Long relates how he goes soloing one day and gets into a position two hundred feet off the ground where he loses control and thinks he's going to fall off and die. The sheer waste of it all is there with him in a flash. Somehow he makes it to the top of the climb and safety, but it has taken a crisis as big as that to make him aware of the only blasphemy: 'to wilfully jeopardise my own existence'.

But whether or not it is a blasphemy – and the question is unchanged whether you interpret blasphemy as something evil, something tragic, or merely as something unwise – surely depends on subsequent events. Long came down from his close shave filled with a sense of joy in the world, and wandered through the meadows delighting as never before in the birdsong and flowers, the ordinary things. That is what one would expect. But the crux is whether it stays like that or whether in a few months one is back at the start and doing the same thing again. The first time is happens: no, that's no blasphemy. The second or third time? Perhaps not. But the hundredth . . .?

The grand old men of mountaineering have all been damned lucky. They have carried out the blasphemy a few times, got away with it, and got out of it, usually to mountain walking in the end. Lord Hunt is a fine example. To the man in the street, and to many mountaineers too, Hunt is a career public servant, an upright and utterly respectable establishment figure who masterminded the ascent of Everest and saw it through with military efficiency. But this is as incomplete as dismissing Bonington as a smooth media man. Hunt is urbane and comes from a family with a tradition of distinguished public service, but he is not the archetypal military figure. He is a typical mountaineer – meaning he has his anarchic streak and has had countless close shaves on small adventurous private expeditions of his own, just like all those nineteenth century establishment figures who spoke constantly of the overriding importance of safety and then promptly went and stuck their necks out. Hunt has done just the same, and knows he has been lucky, rather than particularly clever, to get away with it. That makes him both humble and more able to appreciate the gentler illumination. In his autobiography *Life is Meeting* Hunt recalls his close shaves, but talks also of a 'climate of feeling' which he gains simply by being amongst mountains:

> These experiences are not the stuff of newspaper headlines; they are not identified with any particular mountain occasion. I have found them everywhere: in Snowdonia and Glencoe as much as in the Pyrenees, the Tatras and the Himalayas. Nor are they peculiar to steep places such as these . . .

It seems to me that Hunt's 'climate of feeling' is natural piety. But whatever it is, the significance is that these lines form the last paragraph of his book.

The Lord Hunt of Llanfairwaterdine, now in his 80s, who followed his very
public leadership of the ascent of Everest in 1953 with many private, informal
climbing adventures of his own.
(Photo: John Cleare, May 1973.)

'Humanity coming to terms with the hills.' Gimmer Crag, Great Langdale and Little Langdale beyond, from the slopes of Pike o' Stickle, English Lake District. *(Photo: Peter Hodgkiss.)*

8 Against the Grain

Theoretical studies of mountaineering have generally received a bad Press. Mountaineering is something to do rather than talk about, and theorising can easily become a wish to find common threads and a neat consistency that in reality does not exist.

And then mountaineering is to many people a spiritual undertaking, and anything of worth of that kind is deeply private. Attempts to delve into it may be regarded as an affront. When Tilman said that all self-respecting mountaineers should shudder whenever they see anything about mountaineering in the newspaper, he was expressing a widespread sentiment. That 'information' is now so prevalent doesn't alter it for a moment. Personally I am ambivalent about not only newspaper reports but mountaineering magazines too, and I cannot be the only one.

All the same, I think these studies have to be made; if not this one, then others. Mountaineering goes against the grain of so much of life that preserving it demands more than *laissez-faire*. We know that there is something valuable about it which is vulnerable and under threat – from progress, from normality, from something – in a way which most sports and pastimes are not, and to have any hope of countering the threats we must surely analyse the game, even if the only result is to show us how much must remain a mystery. That, at least, can be the only excuse for a book of this kind.

Why do people go to the mountains? *Because they cannot find a full and lasting satisfaction from ordinary life.* We are told that people take mountaineering too seriously – so seriously that they write philosophical books. But that is not a criticism of them, nor of mountaineering. It is a reflection on 'normal' life. Climbing mountains is a form of protest, and this makes its integrity all the more difficult to hold on to.

The threats come from a variety of directions, including improvements in equipment; the exploration of new areas and the completion of new climbs, removing yet more pieces of the mystery; the gradual destruction of the environment; the seemingly inexorable increase in the number of people involved; the loss of the private dimension resulting from the increase in media interest; and the constant worry of control from 'outside'.

There cannot be many mountain lovers who have not sometimes felt a sense of despair. I remember visiting the Braeriach corries in Scotland one winter, hoping to climb. Somewhere on these slopes is the only 'permanent' snowpatch in Britain, said to have melted only half a dozen times in the last fifty years. I have never visited the corries in summer, but I imagine it as a place of tough grasses and grey granite boulders, where you can almost smell the last remnants of the ice age. I trudged up a high valley in a cold dawn, until the sun melted the snow off the boulders to leave dry lichen warmed by the sun. Overhead was a washed blue sky, and in every direction silence as clear as the sharp air. At the Pools of Dee small cornices overhung the edge and fell occasionally to hit the water with a loud 'plop'. Traversing round a hillside, I finally reached the corries – to find company, a group of survival course students and their instructors. And with that, something absolutely vital was lost. Even the magnificent scenery could not redeem it.

Yet none of this is really new. Perhaps the most striking feature of mountaineering history is not the constancy of the rewards but the unchanging nature of the problems and drawbacks. In 1913 Bourdillon, whose 'moments' remain the goal of every generation, was only one of a continuous stream of writers who questioned whether the essence of the thing could survive. And some of the problems were self-inflicted:

> Surely it was a fatal hour when the enthusiast of mountain-climbing first took to printing – and illustrating – his enthusiasm! Many of us – even I myself – have followed his suicidal example.

Bourdillon believed that overcrowding and the destruction of mystery had already reached crisis point eighty years ago. The great days of Ulysses roaming in worlds romantic and unknown were gone, and things were going rapidly downhill.

But then it's difficult to find a time when they have not been. Even in the mid-nineteenth century, Leslie Stephen thought the summer Alps too crowded for comfort. We have all felt the same – every mountaineer since the beginning of time. Things are never what they were. 'On the Matterhorn or the Jungfrau, on the difficult rock or dangerous ice-slope, even in the mountain hut, how often have we met persons of both sexes who were certainly not in their right place – wherever their right place might be ...' The snobbery masks an entirely serious sentiment: whoever these people might be, there are too many of them.

Mountaineers are ambivalent about progress, and the ambivalence is timeless. Many Scottish climbers opposed the introduction of crampons for winter climbing in the 1950s, and there is the famous occasion in 1882 when Conway and a companion were admiring the virgin Dent du Geant in the Mont Blanc range and discussing the problem of climbing it. Suddenly they realised they could see figures approaching the top. They were witnessing the first ascent, only made possible by the use of pitons, ladders and other technical paraphernalia. 'Thus does the glory of a peak pass away. All the dragons are driven from the Alps and maiden tourists sport in their dens', sighed Conway. Every success is a two-edged sword, even your own. Mallory, endlessly unsure and endlessly expressing it – 'it is not always an undiluted pleasure to hear of new ascents in the Alps, or even in Great Britain' – has emerged as a classic case of doubt.

The environment too has been on the edge of final destruction since mountaineering began. For Bourdillon it was symbolised by the suggested construction of a mountain railway up the Matterhorn. But even before this, in the mid 1800s, anyone who had been climbing for more than a few years was liable to develop a pessimistic streak. In 1862 Josiah Dwight Witney, creator of the geological survey of California, set out to climb the snow-covered Mt. Shasta, a Californian peak which was locally believed to be the highest in the United States. The mountains of the western States cover a huge area and their exploration had at that point hardly begun. One might reasonably suppose that Mt. Shasta in 1862 would have been unspoilt. But apparently not. When Witney and his companion William Brewer got to the top, 'there was a liberal distribution of 'California conglomerate', a mixture of tin cans and broken bottles, a newspaper, a Methodist hymnbook, a pack of playing cards, an empty bottle, and various other evidence of a bygone civilization'.

Today there are many worrying trends, from litter on footpaths to the mushrooming of holiday homes and the destruction of forests. And then we think that people behave less well than they used to. One of my own pet hates is the playing of radios, environmental pollution if ever there was any. But in the 1920s Ivan Waller, now widely revered as one of the grand old men of British climbing, made the first ascent of Belle Vue Bastion in Wales to the sound of a wind-up gramophone. Is there any difference?

We think of the problem of control as new too: the difficulties American mountaineers have with their national park bureaucrats, the constant wrangles in Britain over outdoor education, or the newspaper outcry whenever there is a particularly nasty mountain accident. Yet control, rules, outside interference in general, has always existed, and the problem is as well demonstrated by the Chamonix of the early nineteenth century as by any contemporary Achilles heel. After Mont Blanc was climbed in 1776, Chamonix began to attract an increasing number of visitors intent on repeating the ascent. Whilst these numbers remained small no official organisation seemed necessary. There were only a handful of guides and only a handful of wealthy tourists, and contact between the two was made informally. But after the Napoleonic Wars tourism increased by leaps and bounds, and in 1823 the *Corporation des Guides* was formed in Chamonix. It started with a formidable list of rules and regulations covering the employment of guides and their pay and, in the way of all bureaucracies, the list grew. It laid down tariffs and the number of guides that must be taken on any particular excursion, and by the 1850s no less than four were required for each 'tourist' for the ascent of Mont Blanc. The cost was correspondingly high. Serious mountaineers were up in arms, and one of the first things the English *Alpine Club* did after it was formed in 1887 was to lobby to have the rules amended.*

The *Corporation* was the first association of mountain guides in the world's first mountain resort, and not without value. It provided insurance policies for the professionals (though this did not happen until late in the century and the early guides all relied

---

*See, for example, *Peaks, Passes and Glaciers*, First Series, (1859), particularly the Preface and 2nd appendix.

on the largesse of their employers if they suffered injury); it ensured reliability in the supply, if not the quality, of guides; perhaps most importantly, it provided for the casual tourist who wanted to climb something, anything, though preferably what everybody else climbed, and who made no claims to expertise.

But its relationship to serious mountaineering was less happy. The pioneers disliked being told what to do, they disliked the bureaucracy, and they disliked being fobbed off with whichever guide had reached the top of the guides' rota, not to speak of having to employ four guides, irrespective of their expertise or that of their employer. One is glad to be able to say that they proceeded to behave as any self-respecting mountaineer should, and avoided the regulations whenever possible. Many had formed relationships with particular guides whom they both respected and valued and had no intention of taking on some unknown instead. They generally got their way by using a loophole in the regulations; by engaging their guides outside the confines of the Chamonix valley and then travelling there by foot, the rota could be by passed. When Wills first employed Auguste Balmat in 1853, the year before their Wetterhorn ascent, he used this ruse. Twelve years later, when the regulations had supposedly been amended, it still saved time and trouble. A month before the Matterhorn climb of 1865 Whymper was climbing with two Swiss guides, one of whom was Christian Almer. They had their eye on the Aiguille Verte above Chamonix, one of the few major peaks still unclimbed and one of the most difficult in the Alps. They approached from Switzerland over a col, and were up and down the mountain almost before Chamonix knew what was happening. As with Wills and Balmat a decade earlier, the Chamonix establishment was not amused. There is good evidence, however, that Balmat and Almer were as amused as their employers; another sign, if any were needed, of the spirit which motivated the best of the early guides and which went far beyond material considerations.

Mountaineering at its best is only possible if one is in charge – hence the attraction of small expeditions. Describing the Kangchenjunga climb Peter Boardman leaves us in no doubt that it was precisely because of the expedition's small informal character, paid for almost wholly out of their own pockets, that he felt free and in control of his own destiny in a way he had not been able to do on a much larger expedition to the West Ridge of K2 the previous year. It was the same satisfaction that the West Wall of Changabang offered after the South-West Face of Everest; the satisfaction of freedom and self-determination and a clear sense of who one is. Boardman is acutely aware of how easily it can all be spirited away by external obligations, particularly for a star, performing at the game's frontiers. He wants to be his own man, but the bigger the expedition, the harder it is to pull it off.

And I wonder if something similar does not apply to the more modest case of the modern trekker. Can one of those package holidays which organise everything for you, take away all the worries, all the risk, and leave you no decisions to make for yourself, really deliver the goods? Many people who have got used to walking holidays on their own or with a few friends find that it cannot, and that having no decisions to make merely leaves one feeling small and superfluous. Organising your own trek is hard work and worrying, but there may be rewards there that are not available to the agency trekkers. Agency trekking is sightseeing and good exercise and can be very rewarding, but it is rarely mountaineering in the full sense of the word. One of mountaineering's great rewards is to renew one's sense of self-identity, and it seems that only a 'traditional' approach, with all its disadvantages and inefficiencies, can achieve this fully. Anything which misses that misses the root.*

Because they have always worried the mountaineering world, these doubts can seem rather hollow. The hills get more and more crowded, yet we still enjoy ourselves. One suspects that if the Victorians could have known how many people would invade the mountains in the late twentieth century, if they could have seen the environmental destruction and the amount of information at our fingertips, they would have shaken their heads sadly and prophesied: 'Of course, when that happens everyone will give up.' And they would have been wrong. So can any of the doomsters be taken seriously?

I believe yes; there are trends and events which can ruin mountaineering completely. At the same time it is true that many of the concerns of every era are spurious, being merely the birth-pains of some new style. The great need – the *only* need – is to separate these out so that those things which genuinely challenge mountaineering's integrity can be seen clearly.

If mountaineers are forever preaching doom and gloom and yet Armageddon never arrives it can only be because much of what seems worrying is not in the outside world at all but is built into the very nature of what they do and love. In which case it is hardly surprising that crises of integrity occur with monotonous regularity. Indeed, if there were no crises something would be wrong!

The best example of this is our view of change. When old men write that mountaineering is not what it was, what they are complaining about is change. It is not what the change is that matters; it is the fact that things are changing at all. This cannot be dismissed, because although one of the reasons we dislike change is sheer laziness, another is that in a very real way change undermines the spiritual life, and that is a very good and serious reason for objecting to it. Why do we go to the hills? To get away from a world which is changing too fast to deliver a sense of continuity. It is no accident that as the world becomes increasingly manic more and more people find the hills a comfort. The lack of change is the very *raison d'être* of the thing, so change of any kind is a threat. Perhaps

---

*W. H. Murray, for example, has recently tried and failed to recapture the essence of mountaineering through agency trekking. 'The relaxation won was the wrong kind. One could be happy, know enjoyment, feel at peace, but the real magic was not experienced. Like 'Providence' or all the other intangibles that yield little to scrutiny, the magic of the present moment has to be won on initiatives taken by oneself, and in the sweat of one's own brow, with attendant discomforts and dangers. The reward is for him who accepts the penalty.' (From *Present Moments*, in *The Alpine Journal*, Vol 86, 1981)

that was another element in Tilman's dislike of newspapers; he wrote books, but then books, good ones at any rate, stand outside time. Newspapers on the other hand are a brutal reminder of the impermanence of things.

But if that was all there was to it then mountaineers facing change would be angry, single-minded and determined, and that is not the feeling that is conveyed. What is conveyed is *angst*, an uncertainty and heart-rending rather than a single clear view. The reason is that mountaineering is not only about the unchanging but also about the new, and change is at the heart of that. So our feelings are always contradictory and cannot be otherwise.

And this should be enough to dispose of many of our worries. When we look back and recall, say, the reactionary attitudes of The Alpine Club in the 1930s, we can say: those attitudes were understandable, but mistaken. Though we hate change the very nature of mountaineering demands it and the only alternative, stagnation, is worse.

But this will not dispose of everything. There still remain certain elements of mountaineering which cannot be changed without being destroyed.

The chief of these, surely, is natural piety. There is something in the mountain environment and the way we operate there whose gift is a feeling of belonging and rightness regained, and there is a point beyond which that feeling disappears. Can you feel it in the English Lake District? Most of the time, yes. Can you feel it in Langdale on an August Bank Holiday? I say no.

We can take an extreme situation like that, agree that if all the world's mountains were like Langdale on an August holiday things would have gone too far, and still not worry about it, because we have not yet reached that point. Even today, when things are more crowded than they used to be, there is still plenty of ground to play for, and if you dislike one place you can move on somewhere else. If Langdale has lost its charm, go to Nepal. If the Everest trek is crowded, go to Patagonia, or Assam. But that way out of the problem cannot last for ever and sooner or later it will be impossible to duck the vital question: *what are the essential qualities needed to preserve natural piety?*

One reason this is so difficult to answer is that what we love and hate in the environment is conditioned by personal associations, by cultural history, temperament, and a thousand factors we can never define. It is as difficult a problem as being objective about mountain beauty, and has a great deal in common with it. Certainly it is not simply a matter of getting rid of the signs of human interference. We love the Lake District, yet the signs of our involvement are everywhere.

Natural piety depends not only on what the environment looks like but on the number of people who are in it, and there are reasons for thinking that in the end numbers may be the more important factor. Perhaps Dr Johnson was right; perhaps the Scottish Highlands really *are* rather awful, and the only reason we like them is that they are so much emptier than the rest of Britain. It is very difficult to say anything explicit about visionary landscape – *except that it mustn't be crowded.* We start with the English Lake District in the eighteenth

Loch Coruisk and the Black Cuillin, Britain's finest mountains, on the Isle of Skye. In the late twentieth century scenery such as this is not only celebrated, but loved. Perhaps it would take as much strength of character to hate this view today as it took in the seventeenth century to love it. *(Photo: John Cleare.)*

century, move to the Alps in the nineteenth and end up in the Himalayas in the twentieth, in each case struggling to justify our new-found love with new aesthetic criteria. But really, it's absurdly simple: it's the emptiness we want.*

In 1970 Galen Rowell wrote an interesting article about his first visit to a valley in California called Hetch Hetchy. Hetch Hetchy is only about 40 miles from Yosemite National Park and within reach of a huge number of urban Americans. Like Yosemite, it was for many years untouched and breathtakingly beautiful, with meadows of wild flowers, great granite cliffs and fabulous waterfalls. Then San Francisco found itself short of drinking water and Hetch Hetchy was dammed, despite everything John Muir could do to stop it.

Rowell went to Hetch Hetchy to climb with this dismal knowledge in the back of his mind, but once there he had to start reconsidering fast. The climbing was superb, yet he and his partner had the place to themselves. There were few sightseers, and those few drove up to the dam, got out of their cars to look, and went no further. So – heresy of heresies! – perhaps the dam was not such a bad thing after all? It discouraged people. They went to Yosemite instead, and Hetch Hetchy was left in peace.

> I tried to reassure my old beliefs by repeating to myself, "Hetch Hetchy was ruined; Yosemite Valley was saved. Hetch Hetchy was ruined; Yosemite Valley . . ."

If crowds destroy natural piety, the problem may prove self-regulating in the end. Sooner or later the sheer number of people using the mountains for pleasure will dampen the attraction and some will then turn to other things. In the last few years I for one have refrained from visiting English hills on Bank Holidays, and presumably others have too. Twenty years ago one would not have thought twice; today the self-regulation has begun.

But there is a problem which is even more worrying: regulation and control. There have always been attempts to control mountaineering, and mountaineers have generally resisted them more or less successfully; but the image of 1984 still has to be taken seriously because, as in Orwell's novel, power to control comes from technological advance and this is inexorable. And the most insidious form of control is not control of one's actions but of one's values and aspirations. Television and other aspects of communications technology open up possibilities of manipulation of a new order, in which mountaineers play to the cameras and compete against their better judgement.

I doubt if cricketers or golfers feel threatened by 'society', so why do mountaineers? Because mountaineering operates from a different philosophical base, and the threat goes both ways.

The obvious example is physical risk. Mountaineering has one view of risk, our modern

---

*For discussion of this subject see, for example, chapter 6 of the climber and poet Michael Roberts' *The Estate of Man*, Faber and Faber, 1951.

culture has another, and the result is a cold war. The mountaineer's view is that risk is necessary if we are to love life. Just as Wilson could not appreciate anything until the lorries he was travelling in threatened to break down, so we remain asleep and oblivious to life until someone or something threatens to take it away. It may be a dreadful flaw in human nature, but there it is. Bourdillon's 'moments' and a degree of risk go together. And given that death is the only certainty, which is more important: to search for those moments, or to avoid risk at all costs? Whether one takes an old-fashioned explorer like Shipton:

... nothing can alter the fact if for one moment in eternity we have really lived

or a modern climbing star like MacIntyre:

It is better to live one day as a tiger than a hundred as a sheep

the mountaineer's view is clear; you cannot have it both ways, at least to start with.†

'Society' does not have an answer to that. It has not found a way to make us into saints or even into reasonably worthwhile human beings without our suffering for it. And whilst it claims to believe in the value of the individual, it regards any risky undertaking – one of the very things that can help to make the individual worthy – in a black light. Mountaineering and death can live together, because mountaineering is about a regained primitivism and one of the core elements of that is a lessened sense of the individual ego. That does not make death trivial, but it does make it less than the total disaster it would otherwise be. But in modern life we do not accept the primitivist value system, and we try to persuade ourselves that anything is better than death, even living as a vegetable.

These trends are most developed in America; so much so that climbers there are even protected against themselves. *You* may want to take risks, but that isn't good enough.

---

†Francis Fukuyama's *The End of History and the Last Man* casts an interesting light on this question of a 'cold war'. On Fukuyama's thesis the heroic Germanic philosophical tradition, exemplified by Hegel and Nietzsche, is vital to an understanding of modern man. The key is the struggle of the individual for recognition – *thymos* as Plato had it, or in the most general sense, dignity – whose most fundamental manifestation is man's willingness to die for an ideal or cause. 'For by risking his life man proves that he can act contrary to his most powerful and basic instincts, the instinct for self-preservation. ... And that is why it is important that the primeval battle at the beginning of history be over prestige alone, or an apparent trifle like a medal or a flag that signifies recognition. The reason that I fight is to get another human being to recognise the fact that I am willing to risk my life, and that I am therefore free and authentically human.' Because of *thymos* there is doubt as to whether purely economic man, rational, guided by prudence, will in fact *be* the 'last man'; and if he is, whether he will not be incomplete as a human being, lacking in the fire which alone creates all that is best and worst in human experience.

These general speculations come close to defining much more particular concerns over mountaineering and its future. The nature of *thymos* and its uneasy relation to other aspects of the soul are at the root of any real understanding of what mountaineering has been and might become.

Life is sacrosanct, and litigation is a better persuader than philosophy. Such a situation is totally at odds with mountaineering, and has left many American climbers understandably angry and bewildered. What next?

It is as if people who risk their lives are being more than a nuisance; they are questioning the very basis of society. They are being anarchic. They are giving free reign to their lesser instincts. They are standing in the way of Full Social Adaptation. And this is unsettling. The distinguished journalist Jan Morris, who has often reported on mountaineering affairs, has commented:

> It is as though the mountains are only an excuse: that all your bold adventures, your comradeship, your trappings of mystical guff, only mask something paler and more muted at the heart of you. Perhaps death has something to do with it, standing as it does at the foot of every cliff. Certainly, to this one outsider, the most haunting and nagging thing about the company of mountaineers is a streak in them of a kind of nihilism – something less frivolous than escapism, less sententious than anarchy, less specific than religion.*

If this is right, the philosophical difficulties which beset the outdoor education movement are hardly surprising. Modern education is about social adaptation. Mountaineering seems to be about selfishness, danger, and perhaps anarchy. How can the two go together? Well, one can use mountains to teach people about teamwork, about beautiful places and about their own abilities, and all of this is very worthwhile. But one is not teaching them about mountaineering in its entirety, and trying to do so is strictly for heroes. One's heart warms to Robert Irving, who in his capacity as a schoolmaster at Winchester at the turn of the century took some of his pupils climbing (one of them was George Mallory), and got much criticised for his trouble. What if something went wrong?

Perhaps the problem lies at an even deeper level, with our very modes of thought. The astronomer Fred Hoyle spoke more wisely than many mountaineers have done when he addressed The Alpine Club twenty years ago:

> Mountaineers are always being asked *why* they climb mountains and I am always surprised when they allow themselves to be trapped into offering reasons. The truth of the matter is surely this. Any purpose that can be precisely explained is always temporary . . . It is a curious paradox of human existence that purposes which can be clearly defined and explained have a limited life-span. And conversely, the things in life that last indefinitely cannot be explained and defined.

---

*There is also the question of whether mountaineering is not at root an unavoidably masculine pursuit. See, for example, Morris's incomparable *Conundrum*.

This makes perfect sense. One of the reasons for thinking mountaineering a noble pursuit is that it defies our attempts to categorise it and explain it away. And that is something which the modern mentality finds hard to accept. The religious mentality would feel precisely the reverse of course – that if something is out in the open it is bound to be shallow, and that the profound things in life are always and inevitably shrouded in mystery.

What is wrong with the sort of analytical thinking which has brought us 'progress'? Nothing, so long as it keeps to its own territory. The problem is, it invades the whole of life and we try to see the whole of life in its terms. 'Much of the manifest unrest which is now sweeping over the developed countries comes from the pressure of a technological age', writes Hoyle. 'This is cliché. What is not cliché is the recognition that the danger of technology lies not so much in the production of devices and gadgets as in trapping us into offering aims, purposes and reasons for everything we do. And so technology traps us into things that are evanescent and of no lasting satisfaction.'

As Hoyle goes on to suggest, mountaineering does enable one to see just how limited the purely analytical approach is. Yet still we cannot leave it alone. Perhaps anything inexplicable or unpredictable is perceived by the modern world as a threat, to be moulded forthwith into a more straightforward form.

And I wonder if in the end this is not the real danger of the future. Someone or something – the media perhaps, or bureaucratic interests, or just as likely the mountaineering world itself – will not only stick its nose into sacred places but, having done so, promptly start simplifying them. What we have to fear is that our passion will be bastardised and reduced to its lowest common denominator, that mountaineering will be turned into an Olympic sport, competition, glory, money. Well, those are already a part of it, but they are not the whole of it – yet. If they were ever to become so mountaineering would be a much lesser thing than Mummery, Shipton, Boardman and so many others have made it.

'Since happiness is most often met by those who have learned to live in every moment of the present, none has such prodigal opportunities of attaining that art as the traveller.' (Longstaff.)

En route to the former Kingdom of Zanskar, northern India, with muleteer Mohammed Ali, mules, and unknown country ahead. *(Photo: the author, 1978.)*

Bibliography

A complete bibliography is clearly impractical for a book of this kind. The following list includes only those books – narratives, anthologies and other sources – which have been directly referred to and for which full details seem justified. The dates given are for first publication in English. The more celebrated titles are often available in several editions. All titles were published in London unless otherwise stated.

Other than books, the key written sources are *The Alpine Journal*, published by The Alpine Club, London, since 1863, and *Mountain* magazine, published between 1969 and 1992.

Mountaineering books

Alpine Club, (*members of*)	*Peaks, Passes and Glaciers: a series of excursions by members of the Alpine Club.* First series, edited J. Ball, Longman, Green, 1859; Second series, edited E. S. Kennedy, Longmans, 1862.
Anderson J. R. L.	*The Ulysses Factor.* Hodder and Stoughton, 1970.
Bettembourg G. and Brame M.	*The White Death.* Reynard House, Seattle, 1981.
Birtles G. (ed.)	*Alan Rouse: A mountaineer's life.* Unwim Hyman, 1987.
Boardman P.	*The Shining Mountain.* Hodder and Stoughton, 1978. *Sacred Summits.* Hodder and Stoughton, 1982.
Bonatti W.	*The Great Days.* Victor Gollancz, 1974.
Bonington C. J. S.	*The Next Horizon.* Victor Gollancz, 1973. *Quest for Adventure.* Hodder and Stoughton, 1981.
Bonington C. J. S. and Clarke C.	*Everest: the Unclimbed Ridge.* Hodder and Stoughton, 1983.
Brook E.	*Land of the Snow Lion.* Jonathan Cape, 1987.
Bruce C. G. (and others)	*The Assault on Mount Everest 1922.* Edward Arnold, 1923.
Buhl H.	*Nanga Parbat Pilgrimage.* Hodder and Stoughton, 1956.
Conway W. M.	*The Alps from End to End.* Constable, 1895. *Mounmtain Memories: a pilgrimage of romance.* Cassell, 1920.
Craig D.	*Native Stones; a book about climbing.* Secker and Warburg, 1987.
Diemberger K.	*Summits and Secrets.* George Allen and Unwin, 1971.
Finch G. I.	*The Making of a Mountaineer.* Arrowsmith, 1924.
Forbes, J. D.	*Travels through the Alps of Savoy and other parts of the Pennine chain . . .* A. and C. Black, 1843.
Greene R.	*Moments of Being.* William Heinemann, 1974.
Gribble F.	*The Early Mountaineers.* T. Fisher Unwin, 1899.

Hankinson A.	*The Mountain Men.* Heinemann Educational Books, 1977.
Haston D.	*In High Places.* Cassell, 1972.
Herzog M.	*Annapurna; Conquest of the First 8000m Peak.* Jonathan Cape, 1952.
Hillary E.	*High Adventure.* Hodder and Stoughton, 1955.
	Nothing Venture, Nothing Win. Hodder and Stoughton, 1975.
Hornbein T. F.	*Everest: The West Ridge.* Sierra Club, California, 1965; Allen and Unwin, 1966.
Hunt J.	*Life is meeting.* Hodder & Stoughton, 1978.
Irving R. L. G.	*The Mountain Way: an anthology in prose and verse.* Dent, 1938.
	A History of British Mountaineering. B. T. Batsford, 1955.
Jones C.	*Climbing in North America.* University of California Press/Diadem, 1976.
Longstaff T. G.	*This my Voyage.* John Murray, 1950.
Lunn A. H. M.	*Mountain Jubilee.* Eyre and Spottiswoode, 1943.
	Switzerland in English Prose and Poetry. (An anthology.) Eyre and Spottiswoode, 1947.
Maraini F.	*Where Four Worlds Meet.* Hamish Hamilton, 1964.
Mason K.	*Abode of Snow: a history of Himalayan exploration and mountaineering.* Rupert Hart-Davis, 1955; Reprinted by Diadem, 1987.
Matthiessen P.	*The Snow Leopard.* Chatto and Windus, 1979.
McIntyre A. and Scott D.	*The Shishapangma Expedition.* Granada, 1984.
Messner R.	*The Crystal Horizon.* The Crowood Press, 1989.
Mummery A. F.	*My Climbs in the Alps and Caucasus.* Fisher Unwin, 1895.
Murray W. H.	*Mountaineering in Scotland.* Dent, 1947.
	Undiscovered Scotland. Dent, 1951.
	Both reprinted in one volume by Diadem, 1979.
Newby E.	*A Short Walk in the Hindu Kush.* Secker and Warburg, 1958.
Noble C.	*Over the High Passes.* Collins. 1987.
Norton E. F. and others	*The Fight for Everest: 1924.* Edward Arnold, 1925.
Noyce C. W. F.	*Mountains and Men.* Geoffrey Bles, 1947.
	Scholar Mountaineers. Dennis Dobson, 1950.
	The Springs of Adventure. John Murray, 1958.
	To the Unknown Mountain. Heinemann, 1962.
Pallis M.	*Peaks and Lamas.* Cassell, 1939.
	The Way and The Mountain. Peter Owen, 1960.
Patey T.	*One Man's Mountains. Essays and Verse.* Victor Gollancz, 1971.
Perrin J. (ed.)	*Mirrors in the Cliffs.* (An anthology). Diadem, 1983.
Perrin J.	*On and Off the Rocks; Selected Essays, 1968–1985.* Victor Gollancz, 1986.
Pye D.	*George Leigh Mallory: a memoir.* Oxford University Press, 1927.
Roberts D.	*I'll climb Mount Everest alone: the story of Maurice Wilson.* Robert Hale, 1957.

Robertson D.   *George Mallory.* Faber and Faber, 1969.
Rowell G.   *Many people come looking, looking . . .* George Allen and Unwin, 1980.
Ruttledge H.   *Everest 1933.* Hodder and Stoughton, 1934.
Scott D.   *Changabang.* Heinnemann Educational Books, 1975.
and others
Seaver G.   *Francis Younghusband.* John Murray, 1952.
Shipton E. E.   *Upon That Mountain,* Hodder and Stoughton. 1943.
                        Land of Tempest: travels in Patagonia 1958–62. Hodder and
                        Stoughton, 1963.
                        That Untravelled World. Hodder and Stoughton, 1969.
                        A collected edition – *Eric Shipton: The Six Mountain Travel Books* –
                        was published by Diadem in 1985.
Smythe F.   *Kamet Conquered.* Victor Gollancz, 1932.
Somervell T. H.   *After Everest; the experiences of a mountaineer and medical missionary.*
                        Hodder and Stoughton, 1936.
Stephen L.   *The Playground of Europe.* Longmans, Green, 1871.
                        Men, Books and Mountains. University of Minnesota Press 1956; The
                        Hogarth Press, 1956.
Tasker J.   *Everest The Cruel Way.* Methuen, 1981.
                        Savage Arena. Methuen, 1982.
Taylor W. G.   *The Snows of Yesteryear.* Holt, Reinhart and Winston, Canada, 1973.
Terray, L.   *Conquistadors of the Useless; from the Alps to Annapurna.* Victor Gol-
                        lancz, 1963.
Tilman H. W.   *The Ascent of Nanda Devi.* Cambridge University Press, 1937.
                        Nepal Himalaya. Cambridge University Press, 1952.
                        A collected edition of all seven of Tilman's mountain-travel books
                        was published by Diadem in 1983.
Tobias M. C. and   *The Mountain Spirit.* Victor Gollancz, 1980.
Drasdo H. (eds.)
Tullis J.   *Clouds from Both Sides.* Grafton Books, 1987.
Unsworth W.   *Everest.* Allen Lane, 1981.
Young G. W.   *On High Hills.* Methuen, 1927.
                        Collected Poems. Methuen, 1936.
                        Mountains With a Difference. Eyre and Spottiswoode, 1951.
Young G. W. and   *In Praise of Mountains; an Anthology for Friends.* Frederick Muller,
   Young E. (eds.)   1948.
Younghusband F. E.   *India & Tibet.* John Murray, 1910.
                        The Epic of Mount Everest. Edward Arnold, 1926.
                        Modern Mystics. John Murray, 1935.
                        Everest: The Challenge. Thomas Nelson, 1936.
Ward M. P. (ed.)   *The Mountaineer's Companion.* (An anthology.) Eyre and Spot-
                        tiswoode, 1966.

West T.   *Mr West's Guide to The Lakes in Cumberland, Westmorland and Lanca-shire*. W. Pennington, Kendal, 1809.
Whymper E.   *Scrambles Amongst the Alps in the Years 1860–69*. John Murray, 1871.
Wills A.   *Wanderings Among the High Alps*. Basil Blackwell, 1937.
Wilson K. (ed.)   *The Games Climbers Play*. (An anthology.) Diadem, 1978.
Wright J. E. B.   *Rock-climbing in Britain*. Nicholas Kaye, 1958.
Wyatt C.   *The Call of the Mountains*. Thomes and Hudson, 1952.

General

Bell M.   *Primitivism*. Methuen, 1972.
Belloc H.   *The Path to Rome*. George Allen, 1902.
Carritt E. F.   *Philosophies of Beauty*. Oxford University Press, 1931.
Cupitt D.   *The Sea of Faith*. British Broadcasting Corporation, 1984.
Fleming P.   *Bayonets to Lhasa*. Rupert Hart-Davis, 1961.
Frere R.   *Maxwell's Ghost*. Victor Gollancz, 1976.
Fukuyama F.   *The End of History and the Last Man*. Hamish Hamilton, 1992.
Huxley A.   *Heaven and Hell*. Chatto and Windus, 1956.
James W.   *The Varieties of Religious Experience*. Longmans, Green, 1903.
Jung C. G.   *Memories, Dreams, Reflections*. Collins/Routledge and Kegan Paul, 1963.
                   Psychology and Religion. Yale University Press, 1938.
Levi P.   *The Periodic Table*. Michael Joseph, 1985.
McGlashan A.   *The Savage and Beautiful Country*. Chatto and Windus, 1966.
Morris J.   *Conundrum*. Faber and Faber, 1974.
Nicoll M.   *Living Time and the Integration of the Life*. Vincent Stuart, 1952.
Russell B.   *The Conquest of Happiness*. George Allen and Unwin, 1930.
Simon T.   *Riding Home*. Viking, 1984.
Snelling J.   *The Sacred Mountain*. East-West Publications (UK), 1983.
Ouspensky P. D.   *The Psychology of Man's Possible Evolution*. Hodder and Stoughton, 1951.
                   The Fourth Way. Routledge and Kegan Paul, 1957.
Van der Post L.   *Jung and the Story of Our Time*. The Hogarth Press, 1976.
Wilson C.   *The Outsider*. Victor Gollancz, 1956; Picador paperback, 1967.

Notes

All quotations in the main text have been referenced, via a key phrase. Some – early expressions of romantic sentiment for example – have been widely used and in these cases I have tried to give a source likely to be familiar or easily accessible. Several of the pieces quoted are to be found in the standard anthologies.

To avoid confusion between editions I have generally referred only to the relevant chapter of a book rather than to specific pages. Where this is not appropriate the page numbers and the date of the edition used are given. Chapter titles are also included where they are of particular relevance.

On the big hill

'those prodigious lumps of stone'. Loosely adapted from *The Sacred Theory of the Earth* by Thomas Burnet (1684). See Arnold Lunn, *Switzerland in English Prose and Poetry*.

'Cats and monkeys, monkeys and cats, all human life is there'. From *The Madonna of the Future* by Henry James, in *Ten Short Stories of Henry James*, John Lehmann (1948). The context is not, of course, a mountaineering one.

'almost prophetic trance and delight' and associated quotations. These are re-ordered from Coleridge's letters to Sara Hutchinson. See the *Collected Letters*, ed. E. L. Griggs, (1956), or David Craig's *Native Stones* (1987), p 132–3.

'the gentler illumination'. See Somervell's Valedictory address, *The Alpine Journal*, Vol 80 (1965); also Winthrop Young's *Mountains with a Difference*, chapter 9.

'the quintessence of rock climbing . . .' *Rock-climbing in Britain*, chapter 1, first line.

Ranges Beyond and yet Beyond . . .

'. . . realms of dream beyond and yet beyond'. From *Another Way of (Mountain) Love*, by F. W. Bourdillon, *The Alpine Journal*, Vol 24 (1908).

'an infinite number of possibilities'. From *A Sort of Life*, The Bodley Head (1971), chapter 6, section 2. A fuller quotation is as follows: 'I remember an extraordinary sense of jubilation, as if carnival lights had been switched on in a dark, drab street. My heart knocked in its cage, and life contained an infinite number of possibilities'.

'. . . I've at least had some kick out of life'. Quoted by Dennis Roberts in *I'll Climb Mount Everest Alone*, p 88.

'. . . all experience is an arch wherethro'/ Gleams that untravelled world, . . .' Shipton used these words as the final lines of his autobiography, *That Untravelled World*.

'In pride of our humanity . . . we go for the new . . .' and following. *The Springs of Adventure*, chapter 15.

'. . . the acorn falling softly to the forest floor, . . .' *The Savage and Beautiful Country*, p 61.

'. . . I was bound to make the scientific observations and experiments which alone gave value to my venture'. From *Voyages dans les Alpes*, published in French in 4 vols, 1779–1796. Quoted by Noyce in *Scholar Mountaineers*, p 58.

'He seems to have taken pains everywhere . . .' *Scholar Mountaineers*, pp 64–5.

'This is going to be more like war than mountaineering. I don't expect to come back.' From a letter to Geoffrey Keynes, written before the 1924 expedition and quoted by Unsworth in *Everest*, chapter 4. Mallory had written to David Pye in a closely similar vein in 1922.

'. . . the true enjoyment of the Himalaya, most likely to be found at about 20,000ft or less'. *This my Voyage*, chapter 8.

'What is he doing there, and what right has he to throw away the gift of life (and ten thousand golden opportunities) . . .?' and following. *The Times*, leader, Thursday 27th July, 1865. The criticism is of climbers in general, not of Whymper in particular.

'To be too stiff in opinion is a grave fault' and following. *Nepal Himalaya*, chapter 1.

'revolutionary ideas quickly gained possession of the party, . . .' *My Climbs*, chapter 5.

'a bastard creature, . . .' From *Iron* in *The Periodic Table*, by Primo Levi.

'. . . many of the early climbers had been attracted to the sport by reading the books of Whymper and Leslie Stephen and Mummery. . . .' *The Mountain Men*, chapter XII.

'Do I contradict myself? . . .' From *Song of Myself* in *Leaves of Grass* (1855), by Walt Whitman. See for example *Prose and Poetry*, Cambridge University Press (1982).

'affirmation of personality'. *The Great Days*, chapter XI.

'. . . they are but a medium for exploration into oneself'. *Changabang*, chapter 2.

'But what could be more reasonable than finding out about yourself?' From *A view from Camp VI*, the Introduction to *In High Places*.

'I knew a delicious sense of achievement . . .' *The Next Horizon*, chapter 7.

'On the first of the new rock climbs which I made in North Wales . . .' *Mountains With a Difference*, chapter 1, first prose lines.

'The higher we rose, the more intense became the excitement. . . .' *Scrambles in the Alps*, chapter 20.

'I doubt whether you have heard that the great Whymper is about to attack the Rockies . . .' Letter to C. S. Thompson, March 21st 1901. Quoted in chapter 7 of *The Snows of Yesteryear* by William C. Taylor.

'piratical adventurers' and following. From *The Summit of the Wetterhorn*, in *Wanderings Among the High Alps*. The warning – 'One must never shout on the high peaks', and following – was given by Wills' guide Jacques Balmat.

'In order to prevent the remainder of the party scrambling up with undue facility . . .' *My Climbs*, chapter 6.

'the high places of mountains, the great waves of the sea, . . .' Petrarch, *De rebus familiaribus*, liv. iv. Included in Irving's *The Mountain Way*.

'men like Gods'. This is an interpretation of Nietzsche, not a quotation. See, for example, *Thus Spake Zarathustra*, Introduction, section III: 'I teach you Superman. Man is something that is to be surpassed'. See also Wilson's *The Outsider*, chapter 5.

'the knowledge that no pleasure, no improvisation, can permanently mitigate the monotonous burden of increasing regularity' and following. *Summits and Secrets*, Part IV, *The Break-even*.

'The secret of knowing the most fertile experiences and the greatest joys in life is to live dangerously'. From Nietzsche's *The Joyful Wisdom*, Book 4, section 283. Quoted by Lionel Terray in *Conquistadors of the Useless*. The passage is included in Ward's *The Mountaineer's Companion*.

'Man can preserve his dignity only by showing that he is not afraid of anything' and following. From *The Poetry and Humour of Mountaineering*, in *The Alpine Journal*, Vol LII (1940). Included in Perrin's *Mirrors in the Cliffs*, part 6.

'Many die too late and some die too soon. Strange as yet soundeth the doctrine: die at the right time'. From *Of Free Death*, in *Thus Spake Zarathustra*.

'. . . the individuality of the Herr is not considered' and associated quotations. *My Climbs in the Alps and Caucasus*, chapter 5.

'It is better to live one day as a tiger than a hundred as a sheep'. Quoted in the Postscript, *The Shishapangma Expedition*, and contained on a memorial stone erected in the Annapurna Sanctuary after Alex's death on Annapurna South Face, 17th October 1982.

'. . . the most powerful reason . . . is an itch to get to the top of the thing and see what's on the other side'. *Moments of Being*, chapter 1.

'Here were those magnificent creatures of God, . . .' *The Path to Rome*, (1902), p 179.

'The earliest mountain ascent of which any record has been preserved . . .' Chapter 1 of *The Early Mountaineers*, by Francis Gribble.

'I could go on and on like this for years, on and on forever' and preceding. *The Challenge*, (1977), p 196–7.

'. . . I wanted the sensation of strength and capability to go on and on . . .' *Savage Arena*, chapter 4, part III.

The One Crowded Hour of Glorious Life

'The One Crowded Hour of Glorious Life'. With variations, this is a much used phrase. The original source would seem to be a poem by Thomas Osbert Mordaunt (1730–1809) in *Verses written during the War, 1756–1763:* 'Sound, sound the clarion, fill the fife/ Throughout the sensual world proclaim/ One crowded hour of glorious life/ Is worth an age without a name'.

'Freedom from the fear of fear, . . .' *Mountain Jubilee*, chapter 6.

'Too much pent-up energy and feeling, now useless, was thrown back at us. . . .' From *Altitude*, by Pierre Dalloz, *Haute Montagne*, 1931. Included in Irving's *The Mountain Way*.

'we knew . . . that climbing purely for its own sake can give no ultimate satisfaction'. From *The Mountain Crucible – Eiger North Wall*, in *Nanga Parbat Pilgrimage*.

'. . . Those chaps, now, were really getting a bit of excitement out of life. . . .' *High Adventure*, chapter 1.

'to live in every moment of the present'. See the *Foreword* to *This my Voyage*. See also *Present Moments* by W. H. Murray in *The Alpine Journal*, Vol 86 (1981). Murray quotes a letter he received from Longstaff following one of his own written from the Rishiganga, Indian Himalaya: 'You have seen the best – and now understand what I mean by 'living in the present'; just forget all before-and-after and soak the moment into you so that it will never come out'.

'. . . nothing can alter the fact if for one moment in eternity we have really lived'. Final paragraph of *Upon that Mountain*.

'. . . Battle against boredom'. *Nothing Venture, Nothing Win*, chapter 4.

'One hot day in 1954 I was hitch-hiking up the Great North Road . . .' From *Postscript* (1967) to *The Outsider* (1956), Picador edition.

'Recent psychology . . . speaks of the threshold of a man's consciousness . . .' From Lectures VI and VII in *The Varieties of Religious Experience*.

'man will give up anything but his suffering'. This is an interpretation rather than a direct quotation from Gurdjieff. See, for example, *The Fourth Way*, 1967 printing, p 372–3, and other books by Gurdjieff's popularisers.

'Every kind of emotional moment, emotional shock, makes you realise "I am" . . .' *The Fourth Way* (1967), p 114.

'I thought as I lay in my tent how delightful it would be . . .' and following. *Moments of Being*, chapter 12.

'Now I can explain to you how I come to write poetry. . . .' Quoted by Wilson in *Postscript* to *The Outsider*. This appears to be the true sense though not the wording of the original passage. See for example De Quincy, *Recollections of the Lakes and the Lake Poets*, Penguin, 1970, p 160.

'We continued our climb, and had an excellent day on the Grands Charmoz. . . .' *Undiscovered Scotland*, chapter 22.

the 'wild ecstasy' of chill water, and following. *Mountaineering in Scotland*, chapter 8.

'Evidently such is my nature'. From *Three Routes on the Schusselkar* in *Nanga Parbat Pilgrimage*.

'It was all over. Was I really happy? . . .' and the following 'Suddenly everything was so natural that I could laugh about it all; . . .' From *My First Eight-thousander: to Broad Peak with Hermann Buhl*, in Part II of *Summits and Secrets*.

'Throughout the night the storm continued . . .' *Abode of Snow*, part VI (3), *Karakoram*; 'with unrelenting ferocity, and the wind seemed to have some personal malice' are the words of the British mountaineer Tony Streather, one of the members of the 1952 expedition.

'The air was still; absolute silence reigned; . . .' *Mountain Memories; a Pilgrimage of Romance*, chapter 5.

'You'd never work this hard for anyone else, . . .' *Sacred Summits*, chapter 11.

'A child spends hours absorbed in play, . . .' *Sacred Summits*, chapter 17.

'We lay down on the grass amid yellow flowers . . .' *Sacred Summits*, chapter 14.

'They were going to a wedding and stared back at us blankly. . . .' *Sacred Summits*, chapter 14.

'playing to the audience of my mind' and following. *The Shining Mountain*, chapter 9. The phrase is used again, in the plural, concerning the Kangchenjunga climb. See *Sacred Summits*, chapter 11.

'I had three months' grace for rejuvenation, and appreciated the summer with the intensity of a soldier home on leave'. *Sacred Summits*, chapter 15.

'Wordsworth loved mountains, . . .' *Sacred Summits*, chapter 14.

"Back again, eh Alan?" and following. From Birtles' (ed.) *Alan Rouse; A Mountaineer's Life*, chapter 21.

'To the Greek the athlete was the typical ascetic, . . .' *Mountain Jubilee*, chapter IX.

'All the time that I was climbing alone . . .' From *Everest 1933*, by Hugh Ruttledge, chapter VIII.

'. . . Comfort was what I promised myself for ever, . . .' *Savage Arena*, chapter 3.

'Over and over again I asked what I was doing there, . . .' and the following two quotations are from *Savage Arena*, chapter 4. The 'three mountains' referred to are The Eiger, Dunagiri, and Changabang.

'. . . If you desire glory, you may envy Napoleon. . . .' *The Conquest of Happiness*, chapter 6.

'I shared the feelings of the Samurai . . .' *Savage Arena*, chapter 7.

'To experience adventure is to heighten perception'. From *Grand Canyon Climb*, in *Mountain 56* (1977). Included in Wilson's *Games Climbers Play*, part 8.

'rather than being deterred by the ordeal, I realised more clearly than ever before that climbing mountains was what I wanted to do. . . .' *Everest The Cruel Way*, chapter 2.

'Who has known heights and depths shall not again/ Know peace . . .' The first three lines, though not the fourth, which has been changed, are from *Who Has Known Heights*, by Mary Brent Whiteside, in *Best Loved Poems of the American People*, edited by H. Felleman, Doubleday, New York (1956).

'. . . I wished to press forward into that sky recklessly . . .' Quoted in Bonington's *Quest for Adventure*, chapter 11.

'. . . I glanced up at the mighty summit above me . . .' From *The Fight for Everest*, by E. F. Norton and others, chapter 6.

'the suspicion that maybe there was something more, . . .' From *Everest: The West Ridge*, chapter 15.

'"I should be thinking great things," . . .' *Sacred Summits*, chapter 13.

'In this short span . . .' Included in Young's *Collected Poems*.

Return to the Primitive

'There is nothing unusual in the feeling for wild country . . .' and following. *That Untravelled World*, chapter 11.

'. . . since 1983 a ten-foot fang has dropped off a fine steep route . . .' *Native Stones*, section 1.

'. . . when I sit on a six-inch ledge with my feet dangling above a two hundred-foot drop . . .' *Native Stones*, section 1.

'. . . every civilised human being, . . .' Quoted by Michael Bell in *Primitivism*, chapter 3.

'This was mountaineering at its most basic; serious play'. *The Shining Mountain*, chapter 7.

'Our hearts overflowed with an unspeakable happiness. . . .' *Annapurna; Conquest of the First 8000 metre Peak*, chapter 13.

'still blissfully floating on a sea of joy'. *Annapurna*, chapter 14.

'There is a supernatural power in those close to death. . . .' *Annapurna*, chapter 17.

'Eventually I found a snow bank, . . .' *The Next Horizon*, chapter 13.

'As a youngster I was very keen on model soldiers . . .' *Radio Times*, 1st February 1992.

'I was not depressed by my own failure . . .' *Everest: The Unclimbed Ridge*, chapter 10.

'One can still see in the mind's eye the slight figure, . . .' Rephrased slightly from Longstaff's obituary in *The Alpine Journal*, Vol 69 (1964).

'every man, he said, ought to have a profession to fall back on'. *This my Voyage*, chapter 1.

'What a chance! . . .' *This my Voyage*, chapter 4.

'in a minute or two'. *This my Voyage*, chapter 6.

'rush tactics'. *This my Voyage*, chapter 5.

'a sheet of palest granite draped with vast icicles, . . .' *This My Voyage*, chapter 5.

'I've had my peccadilloes, . . .' Recorded by Perrin in his *Introduction* to *The Seven Mountain-Travel Books*, the collected edition of Tilman's mountaineering works.

'Hands wanted for long voyage in small boat . . .' Quoted in the *Introduction* to *H. W. Tilman – Adventures Under Sail. Selected writings of H. W. Tilman*, edited by Libby Purves, Gollancz, 1982.

'. . . the whole scene was eloquent of fundamental realities'. *Where Four Worlds Meet*, chapter 9.

'the change that has taken place in our perceptions of life and death . . .' *Riding Home*, section 9.

'dangerously detached from the basic facts of existence.' *Riding Home*, section 9.

' "Do you do it? Cutting off fingers?" . . .' *A Short Walk in the Hindu Kush*, chapter 20.

' "Somebody's left a boot here," . . .' *A Short Walk with Whillans*, from *One Man's Mountains*. Included in *Mirrors in the Cliffs*, part 4.

'Even though Terry is the most understanding husband I could have, . . .' *Clouds from Both Sides*, chapter 13.

'unquestioning cosmic acceptance . . .' *Primitivism*, chapter 1.

'we are a shepherding people. . . .' *Over the High Passes*, by Christina Noble, chapter 1.

'I then realised . . . on what the 'dignity', the tranquil composure of the individual Indian, was founded. . . .' *Memories, Dreams, Reflections*, chapter IX part ii: *America: The Pueblo Indians*.

'It is this feeling of steadfastness, . . .' *The Call of the Mountains* (1952), by James Wyatt, p 71.

' "Take it to your country. Learn to read it, share it. It is finished here." ' Final words of *Land of the Snow Lion*.

'The sculptured figures of Egyptian Gods and god-kings, . . .' *Heaven and Hell*, p 39.

'To whom the mountain stillness is a song . . .' *Of Stillness*, by C. H. Herford. Included in *In Praise of Mountains; An Anthology for Friends*, by Eleanor and Geoffrey Winthrop Young.

Natural piety. 'My heart leaps up when I behold/ A rainbow in the sky:/ So was it when my life began;/ So is it now I am a man;/ So be it when I shall grow old,/ Or let me die!/ The Child is father of the Man;/ And I could wish my days to be/ Bound each to each by natural piety.' Wordsworth: *My heart leaps up when I behold*. Composed 1802, published 1807.

'I live not in myself, . . .' *Childe Harold's Pilgrimage*, Canto III, st. 72.

'. . . an absolute authenticity of environment, . . .' *Riding Home*, chapter 10.

'I now felt myself to be on terms of intimacy with this wild region . . .' *Land of Tempest*, chapter 18.

'even if there was no view and no technical difficulty, nothing except the simple movement upwards'. From *Over the Hills and Far Away*, by John Emery, in *The Mountaineer's Companion*. The article originally appeared in *The Alpine Journal*, Vol 66 (1961), under the title *The Runcible Cat*.

'A striking figure with the appearance and cultural sophistication of the highly cultivated late Victorian intellectual'. From *The Life and Times of Geoffrey Winthrop Young* by David Cox, *Mountain 47* (1976.)

'Inevitably he was a mountaineer, since climbing is the supreme opportunity for perfect motion'. From *The Nation and the Athaneum*, a lecture of 5th July 1924. Young is referring to George Mallory. Quoted by Robertson, in the *Epilogue* to *George Mallory*.

'about one in five'. From *Men in Action on the Täschhorn*, in *On High Hills*, chapter XIII.

a 'delight of rhythm that may reach almost to ecstasy . . .' and the following two quotations. *Should the Mountain be Brought to Mahomet?*, *The Alpine Journal*, Vol 52 (1940).

'It was made clear to me that neither in the mountain nor in myself had the virtue of my mountaineering lain; . . .' *Mountains With a Difference*, chapter IX.

'We discover that there are degrees of mountaineering difficulty . . .' *Should the Mountain be Brought to Mahomet?*

'Since happiness is most often met with by those who have learned to live in every moment of the present, . . .' *This My Voyage*, Foreword.

Fusion in Diversity

'I had the feeling that I was being watched, . . .' *Many People come looking, looking . . .*, chapter 13. See also *In the Throne Room of the Mountain Gods* by the same author, Section V (4), *Ibex*.

'How many more were there, I wondered. . . .' *On the Profundity Trail*, *Mountain 15* (1971). Included in *Mirrors in the Cliffs*, part 1.

'Yes, it was all over. . . .' *Summits and Secrets*, Part Two: *My First Eight-thousander*.

'Do not destroy the dragon!' This is re-worded. Messner actually wrote: 'I'm worried about that dead dragon: we should do something before the impossible is finally interred.' From *Murder of the Impossible*, *Mountain 15*, (1971). Included in *The Games Climbers Play*, part 4.

'How can I help rejoicing in the yet undimmed splendour, the undiminished glory, the unconquered supremacy of Mount Everest?' From *The First Attempt* in *The Assault on Mount Everest 1922* by C. G. Bruce and others.

'a hateful country inhabited by hateful people'. Quoted in *George Leigh Mallory: a memoir*, by David Pye.

'I sometimes think of this expedition as a fraud from beginning to end, . . .' See Robertson's *George Mallory*, chapter 7. Both this and the previous quotation are included in Irving's anthology, *The Mountain Way*.

'a very good stout-hearted baby, . . .' Quoted by Robertson, *George Mallory*, chapter 9.

'. . . The sherpas would not mind "losing" the money they could earn from expeditions . . .' From *Modesty and the Conquest of Mountains* by Arne Naess, in Tobias and Drasdo's *The Mountain Spirit*. See also Boardman's *Sacred Summits*, chapter 16.

'. . . this definite vision of limitation' and preceding quotation. *After Everest*, chapter XVII.

'The real thing about the night was the feel of it – the atmosphere. . . .' *The Next Horizon*, chapter 1.

'It was a restless, disturbing period for me. . . .' *The Next Horizon*, chapter 2.

'. . . To tell the truth I have only the vaguest idea about theodolites, . . .' Preface to *My Climbs in the Alps and Caucasus*.

'A recognition may begin to dawn . . .' From *A Mountain Mind* by Tom Lyon, in *The Mountain Spirit*.

'long, hard days when we do not know in the morning what the evening will bring'. Rephrased slightly from *Murder of the Impossible*.

'The Face is a strange unreal world. . . . From *Everest is Not a Private Affair* in *Mountain Life* (1975). Included in *The Games Climbers Play*, part 5.

'The sight of those mountains was like looking at time; . . .' *Maxwell's Ghost*, chapter 3.

'The sort of climber I like to watch is the man who knows where he's going, . . .' *Apes or Ballerinas?* from *Mountain 3* (1969), and *One Man's Mountains*. Included in *The Games Climbers Play*, part 9.

'"What is the use of going up mountains?" is a question often put. . . .' *The Ascent of Mont Pelvoux* in *Peaks, Passes and Glaciers*, Second Series, Vol II (1862).

The Religious symbol

'I will lift up mine eyes unto the hills, from whence cometh my help'. *Psalm 121*, King James' Bible.

'. . . The trite comparison between a Gothic spire and an Alpine aiguille is not so shallow as it seems . . .' From *Alpine Mysticism and 'Cold Philosophy'*, chapter IX of *Mountain Jubilee*.

'Clearly, the ultimate fears need to be invoked . . .' *The Sacred Mountain*, chapter 9.

'as solid and imperturbable as a great sage in deep meditation' and the following quotation. *The Sacred Mountain*, chapter 1.

'the penalty for error makes me mindful . . .' *The Snow Leopard* (1978) p 230.

'Have you seen the Snow Leopard? . . .' *The Snow Leopard* (1978) p 225.

'a desperate caricature of fear and grasping, . . .' From *A Mountain Mind* in *The Mountain Spirit*.

'. . . we are moving along a road whose ultimate end is good'. *A History of British Mountaineering*, chapter XIX.

'If I were to invent a new idolatry . . .' Quoted by Lunn in *Alpine Mysticism and 'Cold Philosophy'*, in *Mountain Jubilee*.

'was there not some infinitesimal niche in history . . .?' *The Playground of Europe* chapter II(1).

'. . . beatific visions untroubled by the accidental and the temporary' and preceding. From *The Playground of Europe;* included in Irving's *The Mountain Way* as *The Alps in Winter*.

'I came down from the summit filled with the acute awareness of an imminent revelation lost . . .' From *The Evidence of Things Not Seen*, chapter 22 of *Mountaineering in Scotland*.

'"No, no, *no*," I want to say to him. . . .' *Native Stones*, section 19. The words by Murray in this text appear to be slightly misquoted.

'darkest Africas . . . unmapped Borneos and Amazonian Basins'. *Heaven and Hell* (1956), p 9.

'the sum of our values'. *The Sea of Faith*, chapter 9.

'expressive symbols of states of the soul' and the following quotation. *The Sea of Faith*, chapter 8.

'God highest, man below God, and nature a poor third'. From *Sacred Mountains in Japan; Shugendo as 'Mountain Religion'* by H. Byron Earhart, in *The Mountain Spirit*.

'. . . in at least one respect they were superior to almost all other races; . . .' From *Kailas: A Holy Mountain*, by T. S. Blakeney, in *The Mountain Spirit*.

'I felt in touch with the flaming heart of the world. . . .' From *Vital Religion: A Brotherhood of Faith*, John Murray (1940). Quoted by George Seaver in *Francis Younghusband*, chapter XVII.

'I was insensibly suffused with an almost intoxicating sense of elation and goodwill. . . .' From *India and Tibet*. Quoted by Peter Fleming in *Bayonets to Lhasa*, chapter 21.

'The man . . . was greater than his message'. Quoted by Fleming in the *Epilogue* to *Bayonets to Lhasa*.

'The principle of bodily acclimatisation to high altitudes . . .' Quoted by Seaver in *Francis Younghusband*, chapter XXII.

'The contemplation of any great mountain has an elevating influence upon a man'. *Everest: The Challenge*, chapter IX.

'though the individual mountaineer is entitled to claim he is a better man than he would have been if he had never climbed, . . .' From *Alpine Mysticism and 'Cold Philosophy'*, in *Mountain Jubilee*.

'The mountain now stands there proud and erect and unconquered. . . .' From *The Doomed Mountain*, chapter XXIX of *The Epic of Mount Everest*.

'living at lightning velocity'. *Modern Mystics*, chapter VI.

'intricacies of thought enough to fry the circuits of a computer'. From *Coast to Coast on the Granite Slasher* by Greg Child, in *Rock 3* (1980). Included in *Mirrors in the Cliffs*, first essay.

'the many conflicting I's'. See many sections, all well referenced, of Ouspensky's *The Fourth Way*, and *The Psychology of Man's Possible Evolution*.

'The aim of the mountaineer . . . It is to take the place of the Zen Sage who, having meditated on his mountain, returns home not to teach, not to convert, but simply to show that the man who returns is different from the man who departed'. From *A Poetics of Alpinism*, by Bernard Amy, in *The Mountain Spirit*.

'Do but suppose a man to know himself, that he comes into this world on no other errand but to arise out of the vanity of time . . .' From *The Works of William Law* (1749); quoted by Maurice Nicoll in *Living Time*.

'I came down with ambition fulfilled, . . .' From *A Bivouac on Everest* by Doug Scott, Mountain 47 (1976). Included in *The Games Climbers Play*, part 5.

Conditioning in Time

'. . . there is nothing like a mountain of from ten to twelve thousand feet, . . .' From *The Mountains of Bagnes*, . . . by W. Mathews, in *Peaks, Passes and Glaciers* (1859), by members of the Alpine Club.

'a ponderous, ungainly, ill-proportioned lump'. *The Making of a Mountaineer*, chapter XX.

'. . . they cannot compare with the Alps, the Caucasus, or the Himalaya. . . .' *This My Voyage*, chapter 14.

'not a precipice, not a torrent, not a cliff, . . .' and following. Very widely quoted. See, for example, *The Horrid Becomes Attractive*, chapter II of Irving's *A History of British Mountaineering*.

'They have neither form nor beauty. . . .' and following. Again, much quoted. See, for example, Lunn's *Switzerland in English Prose and Poetry*.

'you have a near prospect of the Alps, . . .' See *Switzerland in English Prose and Poetry*.

'nature would be disregarding its proper laws . . .' From *The Old Queen's Summit Baggers*, *Mountain 55* (1977)

'Savagery pure and simple . . . would, I fear, make me shiver'. From *A Substitute for the Alps*, in *Men, Books and Mountains*.

'Their scale is sufficiently great . . .' *Travels Through the Alps of Savoy*, chapter 1.

'Every Thing that is *new* or *uncommon* . . .' From *The Spectator* (1712). Quoted by Carritt in *Philosophies of Beauty*, section 18.

that which makes 'the mind recoil upon itself'. From *The Sense of Beauty* (1896). Quoted by Carritt, *Philosophies of Beauty*, section 51.

'I am convinced that we have a degree of delight, . . . in the real misfortunes and pains of others . . .' From *A Philosophical Inquiry into the Origin of Our Ideas on the Sublime and the Beautiful* (1756).

"what theologians would call an experimental faith in the size of mountains . . .' From *The Regrets of a Mountaineer*, in *The Playground of Europe*.

'a curious web of subtle fancy and imperfect knowledge' and following. Quoted by Carritt, *Philosophies of Beauty*, section 41.

'the local knowledge here communicated . . .' *Mr West's guide to the Lakes . . .*, second paragraph.

'The view, I suppose, is wonderful, . . .' *The Alps from End to End*, chapter VII.

beauty 'cannot on the one hand be purely physical . . .' and following. From *Letters on the Aesthetic Education of Mankind* (1795), by J.C.F. Schiller. Quoted by Carritt, *Philosophies of Beauty*, section 32.

'that in which the many, still seen as many, becomes one'. From *On the Principles of Sound Criticism* (1814). Quoted by Carritt, section 34.

'Have you ever really wanted something . . .?' From *Jannu-Lhotse Solo*, in *Mountain 134*, (1990).

'No feeling of sublimity. I am too tired for that'. From *Sisyphus on Everest*, in *The Crystal Horizon*.

'At the heart of the climbing experience is a constant state of optimistic expectation, . . .' From *Storming a Myth*, by Galen Rowell, in *The Mountain Spirit*.

'Peter and I waited for the day to break, hoping for the weather to improve. . . .' *The White Death*, part II.

'A Valediction'. *The Climbers' Club Journal, 1973–4*. Included in *On and Off the Rocks*; *Selected Essays 1968–1985*, and *The Games Climbers Play*, part 7.

'Take away my life oh Lord. . . .' Kings I, chapter 19, verse 4, King James' Bible.

'Let us eat and drink for tomorrow we shall die'. Isaiah, chapter 22, verse 13, King James' Bible.

'Passive happiness is slack and insipid, . . .' *The Varieties of Religious Experience*, Lectures XI, XII, and XIII.

'This first bit's tricky, . . .' *High* Magazine, no. 33 (1985).

'Some people have it [the spirit of adventure] in greater measure than others. . . .' From *Adventure by Numbers*, in *Mountain 38* (1974). Included in *The Games Climbers Play*, part 9.

'The ego and the will are the driving forces in climbing, . . .' From *A Valediction*.

'. . . the stone which I push up the mountain is my own psyche' and following. From *Shisha Pangma*, in *The Crystal Horizon*.

'. . . the climbers are lost not in God but in themselves'. From *A Valediction*.

'If you detach yourself and observe it, . . .' From *Up Here, Down There . . .*, in *High* magazine, 1985. Included in *On and Off the Rocks*.

'There can be no classical mountain day without a conscious search for beauty'. *Rock-climbing in Britain*, chapter 1.

'. . . the mountains had been a natural field of activity . . .' *There are Other Annapurnas*, chapter XX of *Annapurna*.

'. . . I was saved and I had won my freedom. . . .' From the *Foreword* to *Annapurna*.

'There are other Annapurnas in the lives of men'. *Annapurna* – the final sentence of the book.

'to wilfully jeopardise my own existence'. From *The Only Blasphemy, Mountain 83*, (1982). Included in *Mirrors in the Cliffs*, part I.

'climate of feeling' and following. *Life is Meeting*, chapter 17, parts of the final paragraph.

Against the grain

'Surely it was a fatal hour . . .' From *Without Are Dogs*, by F.W. Bourdillon, *The Alpine Journal*, Vol 27 (1913).

'On the Matterhorn or the Jungfrau, . . .' *Without Are Dogs*.

'Thus does the glory of a peak pass away. . . .' *The Alps from End to End*, chapter V. Conway is here reflecting, from the comfort of the Hotel Royal, Courmayeur, on his witnessing of the first ascent two years earlier.

'it is not always an undiluted pleasure to hear of new ascents . . .' From *The First Attempt*, in *The Assault on Mount Everest 1922*, by Norton & others.

'there was a liberal mixture of 'California conglomerate', . . .' Quoted by Chris Jones in *Scientists and Surveyors*, in *Climbing in North America*.

'I tried to reassure my old beliefs . . .' From *Hetch Hetchy: First Impressions* by Galen Rowell, in *Climbing 1* (1970). Included in *Mirrors in the Cliffs*, part 2.

'It is as though the mountains are only an excuse: . . .' Quoted by Jack Longland in his *Valedictory Address*, in *The Alpine Journal*, Vol 82 (1977).

'Mountaineers are always being asked *why* they climb mountains . . .' and following. From *On Men and Mountains*, in *The Alpine Journal*, Vol 74 (1969).

Index